T0023038

An Exploration of
Trance Mediumship

An Exploration of
Trance Mediumship

Chris Ratter

6TH
BOOKS

Winchester, UK
Washington, USA

JOHN HUNT PUBLISHING

First published by Sixth Books, 2022
Sixth Books is an imprint of John Hunt Publishing Ltd., No. 3 East St., Alresford,
Hampshire SO24 9EE, UK
office@jhpbooks.com
www.johnhuntpublishing.com
www.6th-books.com

For distributor details and how to order please visit the 'Ordering' section on our website.

Text copyright: Chris Ratter 2021

ISBN: 978 1 78535 957 6
978 1 78535 958 3 (ebook)
Library of Congress Control Number: 2021942800

All rights reserved. Except for brief quotations in critical articles or reviews, no part of this
book may be reproduced in any manner without prior written permission from the publishers.

The rights of Chris Ratter as author have been asserted in accordance with the Copyright,
Designs and Patents Act 1988.

A CIP catalogue record for this book is available from the British Library.

Design: Matthew Greenfield

UK: Printed and bound by CPI Group (UK) Ltd, Croydon, CR0 4YY
Printed in North America by CPI GPS partners

We operate a distinctive and ethical publishing philosophy in
all areas of our business, from our global network of authors to
production and worldwide distribution.

Contents

Acknowledgements   ix

Preface   x

Trust   1

Trusting My Guides   2

What Could Be Achieved?   5

All Mediumship Is Healing

What Is A Guide   7

Grey Horse/Two Moons

Doorkeepers/Protectors   9

Guides   10

Chuckles   11

Kao Chu   14

Jack Webber   15

Valued Healing Team Members   18

Main Guide   20

Henry's Protection   23

Sitting In The Power   25

Another Purpose Of Sitting In The Power   26

Understanding The Vibration   27

Connecting Into The Vibration   28

The Vibration Through Tree Hugging   29

Attunement   32

Trance   34

How Trance Works   36

The Light State (Early Stages)   37

The Middle State   42

The Deeper State   45

Deeper Trance Communication 47
An Observation With Fluctuation Of The Energy 48
Pseudo Trance 49
Trance Recoveries 51

Developing On Your Own **55**
Emotions 58
Itchy Sensation 60
Facial Overshadowing 61
Transfiguration 62

Spirit Children **65**
Spirit Children Activity 67

Spirit Helpers **72**
Teaching The Altered State Of Trance **75**

Séance Cabinet Work **81**
Common Questions
Light Force Energy 83
Elementals In Physical Séances 84
Struggling To Return Back To Your Body
In The Cabinet 86

What Is A Title? **89**
The Start Of My Journey With Healing
Psychic Surgeons Are Physical Mediums 92
Be Honest 93
The Healing Journey Continues
Confirmation
A New Chapter Opens Up In My Development 94
Experimenting With Trance Healing 103
Hot Hands 108

Working With The Public 111
  Reading The Auric Field 119
  Strange Case – Gentleman With Crackling Noise
    In His Mouth 120
  Lady With Growth In The Brain 121
  The Transition 122
  Healing Thoughts 124
  Spirit Technology 125
  Teaching Spirit To Heal 127
  A Young Boy Who Would Not Settle 128

Trance Healing 129
  How Trance Healing Works 130
  Eyes Closed 136
  Eyes Open 140
  Trance Healing Teaching 141

Healing Online 143
Elementals In Healing 154
  My First Elemental Experiences
  Floating Guide 155

Angels Within Healing 158
  Another Encounter With An Angel

Spirit Inventions 161
  Spirit Teaching Me To Understand Healing 162
  Life Force Healing 166

Healing Testimonials 173
Perception Of The Spirit World 181
  Physical Mediumship 183

Acknowledgements

I would like to give my heartfelt thanks to my wife Gail, my daughter Natalie and my son Connor for all their encouragement with them reading early drafts, to giving me advice on the cover. Without their help I am sure this book would still be a distant memory.

To my spiritual guides Harry Edwards, Kao Chu, Grey Horse, Jack Webber, Wee Charlie (Chuckles) and all the other guides and spirit helpers who have helped to bring this book to fruition, I am very grateful to them all.

I want to give a big shout out to Rona Macleod for all her assistance with proofreading and allowing me to say, "It's finally a book."

Finally a special thanks to everyone mentioned within the book for allowing me to share my experiences to make this book a possibility.

Preface

I have written this book with the intention of passing my knowledge and experiences on to those who are seeking to further their spiritual path into mediumship and healing. My hope is that others may benefit from the understanding and guidance given to me through my own spiritual journey.

The writing process has, of course, unfolded with the help of my guides and loved ones from the spirit side of life who have been fundamental all through my development into the altered states of trance and trance healing.

I could never have imagined in my wildest dreams that I would be given such a life changing opportunity to work as an ambassador on behalf of the spirit world. To be working in the wonderful field of trance and trance healing and to be an active part of the energy that they bring forward, to my mind, is an honour and a privilege.

I have never undertaken anything that I do within my spiritual work lightly and have always given 100% in everything that takes place when working with those from the spirit side of life.

I have never been under any illusions in my work with the spiritual realms. I am exceptionally confident in the knowledge that the energy we work with can only come from a higher plane of existence. Some people will refer to this as the "power of God" or the "divine source" and others will know it as the "universal energy".

Through the understanding, love and protection that has been given to me by my guides, I have really enjoyed getting to know some of them extremely well on a personal level. There are also those who work with me who I don't know so well, nevertheless, I trust everyone who comes forward to give service through me from the spirit side of life.

Trust

Trust really must be the key element in everything we do with those who come forward from the spirit realms to work through us as mediums. Trust takes time to build up and, the more we work with them, the more we begin to trust them.

I really don't think that anyone at the beginning of their spiritual journey truly trusts the information that they are receiving from the spirit side of life within the early stages of their development. I do not believe that anyone is exempt from this train of thought. Trust is something that takes time to grow for everyone looking to unfold their mediumship, and patience is also key.

I suppose one of the problems that arises within mediumship is that we are inclined to overthink the information we have received. Whenever a thought or picture is imprinted onto our minds from our guides and spirit helpers, instead of us accepting without question the information we have been given, we overanalyse it which can lead to confusion within our own minds.

The problem we have with the information received is that our logical mind tries to take over within the flow of the information that has been given to us, which usually causes doubt within our own thought process as to what is spirit information and what is in our own minds.

When doubt comes into play with the information received, we can start to become fearful when giving the evidence over to the public. This often happens when we start to overthink and believe that what we have received is our own thoughts, and we may embarrass ourselves by giving incorrect information.

It is important to remember that those from the spirit world will never embarrass you or let you down. They are eager to have you as their medium because you are their channel and voice into our side of life.

The essence of the spirit world is all about unconditional love and those who live within that world are about bringing clarity through evidence of life after death through you, their chosen vessel.

They are intelligent people who know that trust is a big issue with us, and they are very patient with the knowledge and understanding that trust is earned and not given.

Eventually, with time, as your mediumship and understanding of the purpose and intention of your guides and their roles unfolds, then the doubts that you have regarding the information received from them eventually fades as you develop a bond of trust.

When you truly start to trust your guides and spirit workers with the information and understanding that they bring forward to you, then you will realise that this is when your spiritual journey takes on a new lease of life and your mediumistic journey truly begins.

The TRUSTING part of your mediumship with your guides takes time. Always remember, it is one thing to say: "I trust" and another thing to really TRUST them, within yourself.

Trusting My Guides

I would like to share with you how my first book was influenced and guided through the love and trust of my own guides.

My guides and spirit workers had been whispering into my ear constantly for months to write my first book, which is called Mediumship Within. To be honest, I had never given any thought to writing a book and did not know where to start. My guides kept saying to me: "If you write the book, it will be published."

I knew of a few medium friends in the spiritual movement who had written wonderful books about Spiritualism and, after having a few lengthy and in-depth conversations with them about the procedure involved, I was beginning to realise how hard it would be to get a book into print. It was clear that many authors have to go down the route of self-publication as they find themselves being unsuccessful in finding a publisher.

I decided to start writing the book, and within a timescale of about three months, I had a rough copy that was, without any doubt in my mind, written with the influence of the spirit world. "What do I do now with the book?" was the thought I was bombarding my spirit guides with quite a few times a day!

Now this is where things started to get interesting. I had been working with a lady who had visited my healing clinic on a few occasions who had been suffering with a condition called M.E.

The lady had arrived with her husband and, after the healing had concluded, I struck up a general conversation with him about the book that I had written and what to do with it next. The gentleman listened to my dilemma and then he offered to proofread the rough copy and tidy things up for me, if needed.

The couple lived in Dundee and I regularly visited the gentleman and his wife at their home over a period of weeks, allowing us to go over the transcripts and shape the book together.

It was on a Friday evening about 11.30pm and we had just gone over what we felt was the finished draft of the book when the gentleman suggested we send it to a publisher. I remember him clearly saying, "There's no time like the present," and within a timescale of about ten minutes, we had sent a copy of the book to a publisher.

It was a bank holiday weekend, and I received an automated email a few minutes later after submitting the copy of the book. The email stated that the transcript had been received and, if I did not hear from them in a few weeks, then I had been unsuccessful and to check my junk mail.

I remember saying out loud to the spirit world whilst driving home in the early hours of the morning, "WELL, WE WILL

SEE!" as I thought about their message: "If you write it, it will be published." I then tried to put the thoughts of the book out of my head over the weekend.

To my astonishment, I received an email from the publisher on the Monday morning stating that I had passed the first stage of the procedure and now the book would be put to the next stage to be read by independent readers.

I could not believe what I was reading! It was a bank holiday weekend and someone working at the publisher had picked up a copy of the book and had read it. I was totally blown away with this turn of events. I remember putting my thoughts and gratitude up to the spirit world: "I TRUST YOU! THANK YOU, THANK YOU!"

Then the doubt within the human side of me came in to play and I remember saying, "Well, we will see if it passes the next stage." I tried to put what was happening to the back of my mind for the time being.

I received an email on the Friday, four days later, from the publisher. I was unbearably nervous opening the email. When I clicked the email open with shaking hands, it said that they were offering me a publishing deal for my book to go to print!

I could not believe what was happening! With spirit's help and encouragement, I had put my trust in them and they had put their trust in me enabling the book, just as they said, to be published. I was walking about all day as if in a dream. The power of the spirit world never ever fails to astound me.

Here is a wee recap of what they had manifested:

They had orchestrated the right person to come into my life at the right time to help me shape up the rough copy of the book and, with his help, we had submitted it to a publisher. It was then picked up by someone at the publisher on a bank holiday weekend and, within a week, a publishing deal had been struck.

Those who come from the spirit world to work with you will never let you down. We, on the other hand, will let them down from time to time because we are human. It is important that you trust them and the information that they bring forward to you. The problem we have is that trusting them completely takes time but, when that time comes, everything changes for you as a person and spiritual medium.

What Could Be Achieved?

The turn of events which had unfolded with the orchestration of the book led me on the path to start to really think about the spirit world and the guides and helpers who come forward to work with and through me.

I truly started to think about what could actually be achieved through this wonderful opportunity that I had been given by them. I could never have imagined in my wildest dreams what was going to take place with them throughout my mediumistic journey.

My life has completely changed direction for the better, and the possibilities of what can be achieved through the understanding that has been brought to me with the closeness of love and guidance while working with my spirit team has given me the foundations for the work that lies ahead.

All Mediumship Is Healing

This is a topic that seems to be overlooked by many people.

Spiritual healers are mediums who have chosen to dedicate their lives to helping people with ailments and conditions that lie within their emotional, physical and spiritual bodies.

Healing mediums do this by becoming the best channel that they can to enable the energy to flow through them, to help connect into the spirit of the client and rebalance the energy and vibration around the person needing healing.

In my opinion, healing is all-encompassing and all other types of mediumship fall under the umbrella of healing.

Platform mediums devote their lives to giving readings or messages from loved ones from the spirit side of life to people on our side of life. The type of work that they do is no different or less important to what we do as healers. The only difference is the way healing is delivered to the recipient. This type of mediumship is all about bringing healing to the heart and the mind of the person receiving the information.

These mediums develop this informative aspect of mediumship through learning to connect into the energy of their guides and communicators from the spirit side of life. They allow themselves, through time, to become clear channels for those on the spirit side of life to be able to reconnect back to loved ones on our side of life. This reconnection between loved ones helps to bring closure and a better understanding that there is no death and life is eternal for all.

No matter what path of mediumship you are drawn to develop, it is important to always remember that we should all be working with the same intention from the same source. The source is love. Love is the pure essence of the spirit world.

What Is A Guide

A guide is someone who has agreed to work with you from the spirit side of life to help develop your mediumship.

Their vibration will be compatible with your own vibration. What I mean by this statement is that their energy will be very similar to your own energy, which allows both energies to blend together easily.

A guide is not there to hold your hand in everything you do in the physical world. Although if you ask for advice or guidance from them regarding situations in your everyday life, your guides may well answer and help you. It is important to remember, however, that they do not have the right to interfere with everything that takes place in your earthly life.

This does not mean that you can't strike up a loving relationship with them as they are very trustworthy and can become good friends with you. The function of a guide is to help you with the information received, to give you a better understanding and knowledge when working with the spirit world.

Guides and helpers can take on many different types of roles in the spirit world. Some guides will take on the role as our doorkeepers/protectors, some will train to be healers, others will take on the tasks of helping us with communication and others building up the energy.

These are just a few of the things they can choose to do but I suppose the list of things they can and will do is endless. I would like to share a few things that I have come to understand through teachings from my guides as to what some of their jobs are.

Grey Horse/Two Moons

I would like to start with Grey Horse. This gentleman is known to me as my doorkeeper or protector. This is not his real name as he is called Two Moons from the Cheyenne nation.

I could not catch his name when it was first given to me. I can recall the conversation that took place clearly in my mind. I was sitting in my taxicab after dropping off a fare in an area called Harburn, just outside West Calder in Scotland. It was a beautiful evening and I was sitting at the side of the road staring into the night sky.

I had been blending with this guide's energy for many months and had received lots of information from him regarding his past life, when he had lived upon the earth plane, but I had never asked him for his name.

I was sitting gathering my thoughts and losing myself in the moment when my thoughts turned to asking him his name.

"What is your name?" I asked and heard a reply which sounded to me like it was something "moon". I was unable to catch it. I kept repeating over and over, "Blue Moon, is that it?"

Once again, I heard what I thought was "blue moons" or was it "two moons"? "Two Moons, Blue Moons" – what a strange name. I was puzzled to say the least. After allowing my thoughts to become too involved and starting to confuse myself, he said clearly: "Just call me Grey Horse."

The name "Grey Horse" was given to me at the beginning of my spiritual journey by a medium who mentioned him to me during a sitting. The medium said in the reading: "You have a Native American guide who comes forward for you and he brings with him a grey horse." When hearing this information, I automatically assumed that his name was Grey Horse. So even now that I know his real name is Two Moons, I still call him Grey Horse to this day.

One of my first encounters with this guide was when I was sitting in an open circle for mental mediumship. For those who don't know what an open circle is, it is an open development group meaning that anyone can join. You can learn to sit in meditation and open up to the energy of the spirit world to see what information you can pick up.

On this particular evening, I was listening to the meditation music being played and started to become aware of strange-looking shapes appearing in my mind that changed into wriggling bodies that were lying on the ground.

The bodies looked like they had been dismembered and were appearing to be moving about in a degree of distress. One of the wriggling bodies started to move towards me when, all of a sudden, a large figure stood directly in front of me and blocked the image that I was seeing from coming any closer towards me.

The figure who appeared in front of me completely blocked the scene from my vision and I was unable to see anything else. I explained to the person running the group what I had seen as it was all new to me.

I was told that there are certain things we are not supposed to see and what had taken place was that my doorkeeper/protector had stepped forward to shield my vision from what I was seeing.

This explanation made complete sense to me and introduced me to the understanding that I was being looked after by my doorkeeper/protector guide.

Doorkeepers/Protectors

Your guardian angel, doorkeeper or protector is the only guide who stays with you all your life on the earth plane. These guides have usually made an agreement with you (before you were conceived in the womb) to perform the role to protect and guide you.

How I understand the way your doorkeeper protects you, when people are coming forward from the spirit side of life to work with you, is this:

Your doorkeeper is a life force energy, a discarnate spirit. When you offer yourself to be of service to the spirit world to work, then your doorkeeper will connect their energy into your auric field forming a waterfall of energy that expands around you, like a bubble of protection.

Any guide or spirit person bringing their energy forward to work with you from the spirit side of life must connect their energy first through your doorkeeper's vibrational energy, before their energy connects into your energy life force which is your auric field.

If anyone from spirit brings forward to you an energy that is not compatible with your own energy or something or someone's energy that should not be there, then that energy cannot penetrate through your doorkeeper's energy of protection that is safely guarding you.

Grey Horse was one of the first guides who came forward to blend with my energy on my spiritual journey.

When he first came forward, his energy felt immense. It would feel as if my body was growing huge in size and my chest felt like it was expanding outwards to gigantic proportions within the blending process into the altered state of trance.

I have got to know Grey Horse very well over the years through the blending process. The information that he would bring directly into my thoughts by him sharing his wisdom and teaching was fundamental in my development. We have a wonderful bond of trust that has been built up over many years. Although he does not come forward so often to talk through me, I know he is always there with loving protection, looking out for me.

Guides

You will have many guides who will work with you through your spiritual journey. Some of these guides will be with you only for a short period of time and others will be there for the whole duration of your earthly life. When the time is right for them to work with you, they will begin to assemble your spiritual team around you. Guides and helpers can come and go as your mediumship develops. You will have guides who will help you at the early stages of your development.

The work that they do with you and the energy they bring to your energy at the early stages allows other guides and controls who are waiting patiently in the background to come forward to work with you when the time is right.

Eventually, you will have a main guide who will come forward and become part of your spirit team. This guide will help coordinate within different aspects of your mediumship. This does not mean that this guide will be the only guide who does everything for you as you will have other spiritual team members.

You will, however, through time gather more guides and helpers around you who will work with you in all facets of your mediumistic path. These spirit people will be those best suited to guide you through that particular time in your development may it be trance blending, trance communication, trance healing, platform or physical mediumship.

Chuckles

Another guide who is a regular visitor within my spirit team is a little boy called Charlie otherwise known as "Chuckles" which is his very apt spirit name.

Little Charlie made his first appearance many years ago in my home. I used to see him regularly standing at the top of my stairs when I would get home after my nightshift on the taxis. I used to think, at first, that it was my boy, Connor, who I was seeing as he was about the same age at the time. I never thought that this little visitor who frequented my home was a part of my spirit team.

My own boy would see him from time to time and would get rather upset as the little spirit boy would appear to him in the corner of his eye in his bedroom and, as soon as Connor was aware of him, he would disappear as quick as a flash leaving a trail of energy that frightened Connor.

Connor would ask me lots of questions about "ghosts" as he called them. One evening, while sitting in the patio area at our house, I became aware of the little spirit boy's energy and I asked Connor if it would be OK to see if I could bring this little boy forward to speak to him.

Connor was a little bit unsure about what was being asked of him but, as he sat on his mother's lap, I gently started to breathe in and out and could feel the energy of this little spirit child blending into my energy.

"Hello, my name is Charlie," he said to Connor. "I'm sorry if I have frightened you when visiting you and your family. I'm not dead you know, I'm very much alive."

Connor asked: "What happened to you that you are now in heaven?"

"I was playing outside in the street when a horse and cart came along and I was kicked on the head by the horse. That's really all I can remember and then, there – I was in heaven."

He went on to say that he had been in the spirit world for quite a long time and had chosen to stay within the energy of a child for the work that he had decided to do with his job on behalf of the spirit world.

This experience with Charlie took away the fear of ghosts from Connor and helped my son to understand that people in heaven are just like us, normal people with a desire to help. It wasn't until a few years later at a workshop that Charlie made himself known to me as a part of my team.

I was in a workshop for development of physical mediumship and it was my time to go into the séance cabinet. I sat down on the seat, closed my eyes and became aware of a different energy coming forward to blend with me; the energy felt familiar but different.

The energy was alive as if it was buzzing through my auric field when, all of a sudden, I felt a rush of energy coming up from my stomach and into my throat, and then I heard: "Hello! My name is Charlie but you can call me Chuckles!"

He went on to talk to the members of the group in the class making them laugh at every opportunity that would present itself. He explained that he had been working with me behind the scenes for quite some time and his job was to build up energy to help me with my development and the work that lies ahead.

It was not until after that moment when Chuckles came forward that I connected him with the visits in my home as someone who was part of my spirit team. I always just thought of him as a little spirit child who frequented my home from time to time to visit my son.

Little Chuckles is a regular visitor in my trance mediumship. He is very much involved in all aspects within it, creating mischief and laughter to keep the energy up.

Chuckles truly is wonderful fun and helps to encourage the other little children who come forward to visit at our physical development circles. He helps them to touch and gently pull on the hair of the members of the circle and encourages the children to move the objects and toys that we have placed within the room.

Chuckles also makes appearances at my healing clinics. I was working in Turkey when a client came in for a healing. He had written a list of his ailments on both sides of an A4 size paper. I read this extensive list and then jokingly said to him, "Is there anything else you have forgotten to mention?" The gentleman said in broken English, "I have a problem with the haemorrhoids." "Oh! OK," I said. "Please lie upon the bed and we will begin."

Now this is when things started to get interesting. As I started to breathe into the altered state of trance blending, I heard the familiar cheeky voice of Chuckles saying, "Haemorrhoids! Haemorrhoids, I'm going to take a look!" I then said within my mind, "Please, Chuckles, go away, I'm working."

Now when Chuckles makes an appearance, his energy

always makes me laugh and this was not the right place or time for any of that. Things went quiet for a while and then I heard his voice once again: "I've had a look and you are going to have to hit them with a stick." I thought I was going to lose myself at this cheeky comment and it took all my concentration to keep myself from bursting out into fits of laughter.

Chuckles' speciality is raising the vibration and he did not fail that afternoon. He is a welcome member of my spirit team and his sense of humour always brings a smile to my face. It shows me that he is very much alive and thinks on his feet.

Kao Chu

Kao Chu is another one of my guides who has been around in my development for a long time. He is an Asian gentleman who helps with my healing and makes quite a lot of visits when sitting for trance communication. He is a lovely character who brings his own wisdom and understanding on many different subjects delivered with his unique humour which always endears him to groups of sitters.

The first occasion that I became aware of Kao Chu was when I was working with a client. I was in a deep state of trance when I felt the energy of the blend change around me and I found myself looking through my own eyes. When this happens, it is a strange feeling. It feels like you are a miniature person standing inside your own eyes looking out. I know this sounds weird, but this is a feeling that you can experience when working in the altered state of trance.

I became aware of the person who was working through me putting a large, old, quirky-looking box to the side of the healing bed. The person used my hands to open the box and fold the lid over. He reached forward using my physical right hand and lifted a long needle with what looked like little beads attached at one end. He then took the needle and proceeded to gently insert the point of the needle into the client's head. He

14

continued the same procedure over and over, using different-sized needles.

I was fascinated at what was taking place. I watched in amazement at the delicacy of the way he worked around the client's head. There was an abundance of needles sticking into this client's head and then he gently flicked each needle, one after the other. He raised my hands and started to wave them over the top of the needles. There was what appeared to be a mist of energy that was coming through my hands which seemed to react and transfer into the top of the needles.

This procedure lasted for about five minutes and then he started to remove the needles from the client's head. One by one he gently withdrew them, but the thing that intrigued me most was that he did not just fling them back into the odd-looking box. He meticulously placed each needle back into the correct compartment within the box with great care and due diligence.

I then felt this healer's energy starting to retract from my energy and I was no longer standing inside my own eye sockets. I just focused upon my breath and found, after a few minutes, I was back in the physical world. I did not mention to the client what I had seen, felt and experienced during the healing but the client said that he had felt as if someone had stuck needles into his head. This was a first for me with spiritual acupuncture healing and, although no-one had physically touched the client's head, he had felt the procedure that had taken place.

Kao Chu has a character all of his own. He is full of laughter and kindness, but he can also have a serious side which are all parts of his wonderful nature. He is an extremely valued member of my team.

Jack Webber

I find it fascinating how things are put in place by the spirit world long before we ourselves connect the dots.

I came across an advert about a spiritual artist who would

draw you a picture from a connection that could be made with a loved one from the spirit world. I thought this would be a lovely thing to receive – a picture of someone who was dearly missed in my life. I filled in the form and put my thoughts of my grandfather out to the energy of the spirit world to see if I could influence proceedings. I sent the form with the money and waited with anticipation to see how events would unfold.

It was about three weeks later when the drawing arrived. I opened the cardboard tube that the picture had come wrapped in and I started to read the letter that was enclosed. The information that was written on the letter said that if this picture was not of a loved one in spirit, then it would be a guide that you might or might not know.

I unrolled the paper and looked at the drawing – it was no-one who was familiar to me. I was a bit disappointed and deflated at the finished result as the advert had stated it would be a drawing of a loved one in spirit. I put the picture into a drawer in my desk and forgot about it.

I was attending a trance workshop about four or five months later and was sitting listening to the tutor talking about some of his experiences with his own teachers over the years when, all of a sudden, I became aware of a gentleman from spirit standing alongside me.

His presence through his vibrational energy felt strong and I was very much aware within my mind that he was holding something in both of his hands. He was standing there for quite some time, not saying anything just watching and listening. Then the tutor stopped in the middle of his talk and said, "Chris, are you aware of a gentleman standing alongside you?" "Yes," I responded. "I'm aware of the gentleman. He has been standing there for quite some time."

The tutor then asked me to go into the cabinet to see if this gentleman had something to say through me. I went into the cabinet and started to calm my mind through the breath, allowing myself after a short period to go into the altered state of trance. Within a few minutes of the blending process, I could hear the tutor asking everyone to be quiet. "I can see you," said the tutor. "Please come forward stronger so the rest of the group can see you." "Can you see him?" he said to the group. "Yes, we can see him," was their reply.

Now remember, I was in the cabinet and, yes, I could hear the conversation that was taking place with the tutor but I did not know who was blending with me. I felt myself starting to go deeper into the blending and I could feel the spirit person's energy taking more control over my energy. I heard the tutor saying, "Please take more control over the medium and let's hear what you have to say."

The gentleman stated to speak through me and said that he was there to work with the medium (me) and he had come forward to make his introduction to the medium and the group. He went on to say that he was known on the earth plane in his time as a physical medium. I heard the tutor asking, "Are you a guide to the medium?" "Yes, I'm one of the guides who will work with him in this particular type of mediumship."

The guide spoke to the group for some time about development and the hard work that lay ahead for everyone who answers the call to be of service. I could hear the conversation that was taking place, but I could not interfere even if I wanted to. I wanted to know who this was blending with me, but I heard the tutor saying to the group, "Please don't mention if you know the name of this person who is with the medium."

I was then shown a vision in my mind of the picture that I had put in the drawer a few months previously. The drawing which was of the person who I might know or may not know. Then I was shown an image of a picture of a medium from a book that I had read a short time back. The visions were put alongside each other to show me the connection. They were identical, like a mirror image. It was Jack Webber, a well-known physical medium, who was blending with me.

I went home after that experience in a daze at what had happened at the workshop that day. The first thing I did when I got home was to take a photo on my phone of the drawing that was in my drawer from the psychic artist and a photo of Jack Webber from the book I had read about him, and put them alongside each other just to check what I had been shown in the cabinet was correct. I'm not saying that I don't trust what I'm given by spirit, but sometimes the human side of us comes out and it's nice to confirm things for yourself.

The drawing of Jack Webber from the psychic artist takes pride of place alongside the drawings of Henry (Harry Edwards, my main guide) that have been gifted to me and my other pictures and photos of my spirit team who I know work with me.

Jack has become a welcome addition to my development along with my other guides and helpers from the spirit side of life. I often think about what took place that day and I do not know why I did not discard the drawing of someone who I did not know after being so disappointed that I did not receive a picture of my grandfather but, in hindsight, sometimes there is a greater plan at work that we are not yet aware of.

Valued Healing Team Members

There is a spirit guide who works through me regularly when a healing is taking place. I know he was a psychiatrist when he lived in our world. I do not know his name, but I do know that he is present each time I go to work in the altered state. His job is to check the mental stability of the client requiring a healing and to make sure the energy through the connection is compatible with the client.

Another regular guide who works through me is a German gentleman who I know was a doctor when he was on the earth plane. He never generally speaks as a rule and I'm not completely sure of his name, although I believe it to be Robert. Lots of people who have the gift of seeing spirit have witnessed him overshadowing me when I'm working in the altered state with healing.

There are two female nurses who I am aware of being very much part of my spirit team. These ladies work tirelessly backwards and forwards around the room. They assist the healing procedure by laying out and organising spiritual instruments onto silver trays and attending to the needs of the client, surgeons and healers every time a healing takes place.

Their job is no different to what nurses would do today in a hospital environment. One of the nurses wears a great big hat and a white dress like they used to wear in the era around the 1950s and the other wears a uniform that is more up-to-date. These ladies are an important part of my team and help organise what is required from the spirit side to ensure all is in place before and during the healing process.

I have another spirit surgeon who I know works through me. He is a giant in stature, about six foot seven inches in height and wears up-to-date scrubs. I believe he was from Australia when he lived and worked on the earth plane. I see him regularly when working with clients online conducting one-to-one healing.

There are also two lady spirit surgeons who I know work through me. These ladies work with female clients who come with ailments of a delicate nature within the reproductive organs.

These are just some of the guides and helpers who I have shared with you up to now. There are a lot more I haven't mentioned, some I know well and others not so well. They are all part of my spiritual team and, as my experiences unfold with them through the rest of the book, I hope you too realise that the amount of people who can work through and with you from spirit is endless.

Main Guide

I would now like to introduce you to my main guide and leader of my spirit team – his name is Harry Edwards.

Harry Edwards is a very well-known name in the spiritual movement across the world and his legacy is continued through the Harry Edwards Healing Sanctuary. Known simply as "Henry" to his friends, he was one of the most prolific spiritual healers in the last century.

Henry is an energy worker who still works with lots of people on the earth plane today. He made himself known to me, when the time was right, at a workshop which was a few years into my trance development. He came forward and showed me snippets of his spiritual journey and explained how healing was very important to him in his life.

I have covered this first encounter with Henry in my previous book, so I won't go over old ground. It is interesting to note, however, that Jack Webber's and Henry's energies are so similar that I can't tell the difference between them when they come forward to blend with me. They let me know which one is coming to work just before the blending is complete by Henry saying, "Hello, Christopher," and Jack with the more informal, "Hi, Chris!"

I did not cover in my previous book the fact that I had no desire to be a spiritual healer.

Many developing mediums are drawn to healing in the beginning of their spiritual journey. It appears to be very common practice that they start within the healing side of mediumship and then change their direction onto other aspects of mediumship.

For me, it was the total opposite. I had my mind set on becoming a platform medium and, when the trance element was brought forward to me, then I wanted to be a trance medium and I suppose like everyone else, a physical medium with ectoplasm and materialisation.

Although I was humbled, privileged and honoured that Henry had made himself known to me at this workshop, it wasn't until later that I started to think about healing in my mediumship.

I kept saying to myself: "Healing, that's not for me. Why have I been given this gift? I don't want it." These were the thoughts that kept going through my mind. I continued to sit and blend with Henry every day, but I was struggling to come to terms with the healing side of things. Healing really was not for me, or so I thought!

Then one evening while sitting with my friends in our trance development group, everything changed. I was sitting for trance communication when I felt a familiar energy come and blend with me, it was Henry. Henry started to speak through me and, yes, I could hear the whole conversation that was taking place.

I will cover the topic of mediums hearing when in trance later but, for now, I will continue with the turn of events.

Henry started to talk about the importance of healing, what it had meant to him, how it was needed in the world we live in today and how it had started to be overlooked within the spiritual community.

Henry said that the job of a trance medium is to allow spirit, through the blending process, to reach a certain depth with the medium and then they would decide what was best suited for that medium's spiritual journey.

Now I'm not saying that healing has been overlooked in any way within organisations or individuals who have chosen to follow the healing path but what he said to the group that evening was a revelation to me. I understood there and then everything that he had said, and I accepted that healing was my spiritual gift given to me from the spirit world.

Henry and I have become very good friends over the years, and I find myself speaking with him often about general things as well as spiritual things. I never pester him as a rule because

I know he has lots of work that he does constantly on behalf of the spirit world.

It took me many months to eventually call him "Henry" as I always called him "Mr Edwards". He would frequently say: "Call me Henry!" but I would always revert back to "Mr Edwards". Things are different now as Henry has become a true friend over time.

Henry, along with other guides, has been a great support to me over the years. He is always there when I need him, especially when I am a little unsure of what is happening during particular events in my development. I always hear his voice guiding me in times of uncertainty or confusion within my own journey.

I would like to touch upon a couple of incidents when he has been there guiding and supporting me.

I was sitting one afternoon in my home and blending with the trance energy for development when, all of a sudden, I felt myself starting to sway backwards and forwards within the energy as I sat upon the seat. The motion of the swaying backwards and forwards started to gain momentum when, suddenly, I felt a surge of energy that whisked me forward. The only way to explain it was as if my spirit had been flung out of my physical body and I was travelling at an alarming rate upwards like on a roller coaster but a lot faster.

I started to panic as I was travelling forward at what felt like a terrific rate of speed. I could hear Henry's voice reassuring me that everything was OK, and I was safe. He kept repeating over and over, "Everything is OK, do not panic."

Eventually everything came to a stop and I was surrounded with colours that I had never experienced or seen before. The energy within the colours that were all around me felt so peaceful and inviting, it felt homely, as if I belonged within this existence. I was, at that moment, at peace with everything within the vibration of the universe, content with life itself. All of a sudden, I felt another energy take control of me and, again,

I found myself being pulled backwards at an incredible speed.

I could hear Henry's voice once again. He kept repeating over and over that everything was OK, not to panic and just breathe. Within moments, I returned back to the room where this experience had started from and I just sat there in the seat. I felt sick to my stomach. My energy was all over the place. I could not feel my feet at all. My feet were not solidly planted on the floor, they felt like they were under the floorboards!

I really started to panic and, once again, Henry spoke to me telling me to trust, just breathe and everything will come back in due course. I must have sat there for at least half an hour before I felt like I was completely back together.

I have been extremely privileged as I have been taken there now on a couple of occasions and have been informed that this has happened so I could experience the collective energy of the spirit world. Some people would understand this place as "heaven".

What a truly unique experience to be given but, if it had not been for the support and guidance from Henry throughout this extraordinary encounter, then my panicking might have brought about a totally different outcome.

I don't just think of Henry as just my main guide but also a companion and a friend.

Henry's Protection

I was working with a gentleman who had a cancerous condition, and I was conducting the healing session with him at a friend's home. I had just gone into an altered state and connected with the energy of Henry when, all of a sudden, the door of the room opened and I heard someone scrambling over the futon at the rear of me and positioning themselves at the feet of the client who was lying upon the bed.

This person was not invited to participate in the healing and had taken it upon themselves to join in. I heard Henry's voice speaking through me. He said, "Do not touch the patient, please kindly leave the room." There was silence for a few moments and then I heard the person scrambling once again over the futon and closing the door behind them as they left.

I spoke to Henry after the healing and I was told that, when a healing is undertaken, those involved from spirit put certain factors in place to protect all involved in the proceedings and someone coming into the energy uninvited can cause unnecessary complications.

I took great comfort in the understanding that both my client and I were being looked after throughout the healing by Henry and my spirit team.

In hindsight, the lady who did this should have known better as she prides herself on being a working medium.

Sitting In The Power

I would like to make reference to the practice of sitting in the power as sitting in the presence of the divine source, universal energy or sitting in the energy of the vibration of all life. I have sat in the power all through my spiritual journey and it has taken many years for me to understand what sitting in the power is all about.

When I first started my pursuit of trance development, I attended lots of trance workshops over many years in various locations around the UK. I really enjoyed these times in the early stages of my development. They allowed me to meet new people and to hear their personal stories about their own spiritual journeys.

I found that I had a hunger for knowledge that was burning inside of me. The desire to continually discover more sent me on a quest to gather as much information as I could possibly obtain to help me gain a better understanding of what trance mediumship was all about.

At the workshops and events I had attended, the tutors would often make reference to sitting in the power as "the act of blending with the energy of spirit". I took this information from them at the early stages of my journey as gospel.

I find it interesting today that a few of these tutors, who I had the pleasure to sit with as a student at their workshops and events all those years ago, have started to separate the exercise of sitting in the power from sitting and blending with spirit.

Learning to sit in the power is not about blending with the energy of your guides and spirit helpers. Blending with the energy of your guides and spirit workers is the mediumistic side of your development. When you learn to sit in the power correctly, there are many advantages with this simple exercise.

Firstly, our own spirit is connected into the vibration of

life from the moment we are born into the physical world and remains connected when we return back to the world of spirit.

When sitting in the power, you are taking the time to acknowledge the connection that your own spirit has into the vibration of the life force energy, which is all around us all the time.

Doing this exercise is about us taking the time out from our busy lives and connecting into the vibration of the life force energy through the simple motion of the breath allowing our own spirit within, which has a higher intelligence, to be fed through the vibration of life.

There is a greater understanding of the purpose of life that can be obtained within the vibrational energy that is all around us and, by taking the time to connect into the vibration, it enables us to experience it through the growth of our own spirit.

We are here on the earth plane to gain new life experiences. This involves all the highs and the lows that we will face, which all helps with our own spiritual progression.

Basically, sitting in the power allows the spirit within to grow.

Another Purpose Of Sitting In The Power

When developing your mediumship, you may hear some people use the phrase "learning to hold your own power". The power that they are talking about is your own power source, your mediumistic battery source which is contained within the solar plexus area of your physical body.

This battery is where your power comes from for your mediumship, not from your mind. The mind is where the intention is set for what we are striving to achieve within our mediumship which is true connection to spirit.

Sitting in the power enables the battery source to be charged and recharged when it has become depleted. There is no exercise that we can do ourselves to recharge the power back into our battery source apart from sitting in the power.

You may also hear, from time to time, people in the spiritual movement commenting that a certain medium's energy "is powerful". It is important to remember when hearing these types of statements that no medium holds any greater energy or power than anyone else.

The energy and vibration we work with belongs to the divine source and this energy does not belong to anyone, it is freely given to all who choose to work with it. Those who have chosen to sit within the power have allowed themselves to grow through spiritual progression and, as their spirit grows within the vibration, the energy created within and around them emanates more freely through them creating a spiritual presence that can be felt by all. We develop as spiritual mediums to accept the energy within the vibration without question.

Through taking the time to sit in the power, our spirit within is able to connect into the vibration of life and has the ability to become one with its surroundings. Learning to sit in the power correctly takes dedication but is well worth the hard work and effort. Sitting in the power is about learning to still your mind and become one with the vibration that is all around allowing us to connect into the essence of all life.

Understanding The Vibration

When we go for a walk in the countryside or find ourselves standing on a beach gazing out to the horizon, the first thing we normally do is take deep breaths of the fresh air into our lungs. By doing this breathing action, we find that this helps us to relax and bring our mind into harmony with our surroundings.

What we are actually doing is connecting our spirit into the vibration of life. We are not thinking about what we are doing, we are just connecting back into the vibration through the natural process of the breath without thinking about it.

When you sit in the power in your home or in your own little sanctuary, the vibration is no different to being outside as it is also inside. You are learning to allow your spirit to connect back into the vibration of all life.

Now if you give it some thought, your spirit is connected into the vibration of life all the time through the motion of the breath and we never think about it. The oxygen we breathe in carries what is required to enable the physical body to breathe, and the vibration that is carried within the breath feeds the vibration into the spirit body.

We know, without question, that we live in a vibrational world. Taking the time to learn to sit in the power correctly is about us learning to acknowledge that our own spirit is a separate entity to the physical body. It has a higher consciousness of its own and is connected by an invisible silver cord to the physical body.

I find it deeply interesting that all ailments, lumps and bumps that we carry upon the physical body are present also within the spiritual body. The physical body is the shell that we wear when we are living in the physical world but who we truly are is the spirit within.

Connecting Into The Vibration

I remember going for a walk one morning out in the countryside and found myself standing at a lovely grassy area surrounded by trees. I looked about and gazed at the beauty of nature's garden. The trees were full of leaves gently swaying in the breeze and, as I looked upwards beyond the top of the trees into the beautiful clear blue sky, I thought to myself, "This view is bliss."

As I was staring into the blue sky above, a strange thing started to happen. At first, I thought there was something wrong with my eyes; it was as if they were becoming out of focus. The sky was no longer solid-looking in its appearance, it had become pixelated as if it was breaking up into millions and millions of moving particles.

I moved my focus towards the green leaves that were swaying upon the branches of the trees. The leaves appeared to be pixelating the same as the sky. The leaves were not just green in colour, they had become blurry as if they were shimmering within the vibration. I watched in amazement at what was unfolding in front of me, everything around me had ceased to appear in solid form.

I was no longer looking at the world as I had known it, I was now looking at how everything in our physical world was made up through the vibration of life. I was in awe of this new experience, but the strangest thing was that I understood what I was being shown.

The amazing vision lasted for quite some time and then I felt my eyes returning back to normal. This wonderful insight into seeing how solid forms break down through the pixelation of the particles of atom and matter has never left me after this profound experience. It only happens with me when I connect into the vibration of life.

The Vibration Through Tree Hugging

I had the pleasure of visiting the Arthur Findlay College in the early stages of my spiritual development. This is a wonderful place full of beautiful spiritual energy and I would recommend that everyone visit at least once in their spiritual development journey.

I was attending a weekend course for trance development at the AFC and, when I was there, I observed that lots of the students would take the time to go for a walk within the grounds at break times. The students would usually walk at the back of the college and would head down to touch and cuddle the most beautiful-looking tree that stands strong and proud on its own at the bottom of the gardens.

I was sitting thinking to myself, when seeing this take place, that these people must be mad. Imagine hugging a tree! What's all this nonsense about!?

My curiosity started to get the better of me as I watched more and more students hugging the tree. I waited until the cover of darkness to head off down to the gardens towards the tree. I must admit, as trees go, this was a fine specimen. As I cautiously wrapped my arms around it, I noted it had a lovely feel to the bark and the trunk was massive in circumference. I came away from this tree hugging experience scratching my head as to why anyone would want to hug a tree. I just did not understand what it was all about.

Many years after the experience of tree hugging at the Arthur Findlay College, I found myself out walking with my family through the woods at Blackness. While walking, I had this overwhelming inclination that came over me to hug a tree. I said to my family, "I feel I've got to hug this tree," and was given a look of disbelief as if I had lost the plot! My wife and son hurriedly scampered away from me! I proceeded to put my hands onto the bark of the tree, closed my eyes and let myself connect into the vibration around me through the motion of my breath.

All of a sudden, I became aware that the tree had an energy and vibration of its own. It was totally different from my previous encounter of tree hugging. This energy, coming through the connection being made with the tree, felt as if it was alive. I held my hands onto the bark of the tree. It felt that I was becoming part of the tree, as if our vibrations were merging together – becoming one.

I could feel the vibration that had been created start to travel down the body of the tree. I then became aware that the tree was connected through its roots into the earth. The experience did not stop there. I could feel the vibration of the energy connecting through the roots of the tree and into the earth; the energy spread wider and wider in all directions.

The feeling was incredible. I could feel the life in the ground from right under my feet and spreading down to the beach. I was no longer aware of holding my hands on to the side of the tree but now I was conscious of being connected to everything that was all around me. I was, in that moment, at one with the vibration of life. This experience was a life changing moment for me on my spiritual journey.

Although I had sat in the power for many years, it wasn't until this moment with the experience of this tree hugging that I understood the importance of sitting in the power and connecting into the vibration of life.

Another experience I can recall is when I was running a retreat in Ireland. It was a lovely sunny day and I took the students outside to do some trance exercises. The group were quite experienced with the altered states of trance and I had decided to join in with them while they were sitting in the power.

I focused on my breath and went into the peace and quiet and, after a few minutes, I became aware that I was becoming part of the vibration that was all around me. I could feel my own vibration becoming part of the surroundings. My energy was spreading and connecting into everything around me, and all my senses were becoming heightened.

I could hear everything all around me so clearly. My senses were so attuned that I could even hear and sense a small mouse scurrying in the field below. I was part of the wind, the trees and the earth below my feet. I had become one, at that moment, with the universe. It is a wonderful experience to be able to connect and become part of the vibration of life.

Back at home, I was sitting in the power one evening in the comfort of my bedroom. I felt myself drifting into the silence when, all of a sudden, I became aware that I was no longer in my room. I found myself part of the vibration outside. I was listening to a conversation that was taking place between two ladies who were outside my house as they walked up the street. I followed with them listening intently for a few minutes before I felt myself return to my bedroom.

There are no limits to what can take place when we are dealing with the energy of the vibration of life. Sitting in the power is a key element for developing understanding of what can be achieved through trust and dedication – to let go and explore the possibilities.

Some of these experiences I have shared with you are part of my own understanding of what sitting in the power has taught me about the vibration of life on my own spiritual journey.

Attunement

Attunement is one of the most important elements of our spiritual work. To be able to get the connection correct can take time. Never be in a hurry to begin the work, when representing the spirit world, without getting the attunement correct.

You have to allow the energy of the vibration of your guides or communicators to blend into your life force which is your auric field.

It is best practice to attune yourself to their energy before you go to work on their behalf by setting the intention in your mind that you are planning to work and inviting them to come forward and attune to your energy.

If the connection is not stable, then the information you receive or the healing energy you are trying to work with will not be correct for the work that lies ahead. Through time, you will recognise the blending of the vibrational energy of those who come forward to work with you and you will know when the connection feels right.

The attunement process is important for all types of mediumship. To give you an example, when we are asked to send distant healing, we attune our vibrational energy to a helper's energy from the spirit side of life. This person has the job of collecting the information from us and relaying it through the appropriate channels to the right department for healers from their side of life to visit the spirit of the person who the healing request has been asked for on our side.

There is no point in just placing the name of the person who requires healing into the universal energy as the intention is lost with the vibration. Attuning to the helper from the spirit side of life makes sure that the request has been acknowledged and dealt with appropriately through the proper channels.

It is always better to have quality than quantity when working on behalf of the divine creator with the spirit world.

Trance

There are many different points of view and debates today within the spiritual community regarding what trance mediumship is or should be. We know that many years ago it was referred to as "spirit entrancement" and later shortened to "trance mediumship". I suppose what trance mediumship is and what it should be called today is "controlled mediumship". Before I explain the workings of trance mediumship, I would like to explain quickly the workings of platform mediumship.

A platform medium develops to raise or quicken their vibration, and those in spirit learn to lower their vibration, allowing both parties to meet somewhere in the middle for communication to take place through the "clairs" that the medium has developed and so is able to understand the information received.

This type of developed mediumship allows the medium to be aware of the information received that is brought forward to them from those in the spirit world allowing the given information to be passed over to a recipient through the conscious awareness of the platform medium.

These are the five most common "clairs" and what they mean:

Clairvoyance:	clear vision
Clairaudience:	clear audio/hearing
Clairsentience:	clear sensation or feeling
Clairscent:	clear smelling
Clairgustance:	clear tasting

Trance mediumship is a completely different type of mediumship to those who choose to follow the development of platform mediumship. Trance mediums learn to still the mind and allow guides and communicators to speak and work freely through them without their own thoughts interfering with what is being conveyed.

Trance mediums do not develop to raise their vibration like platform mediums. They learn to slow down their vibration to allow the vibration of those coming forward from the spirit side of life to blend into their life force energy (their auric field). Those who come forward to work from the spirit side of life do not enter the body of the trance medium. The two vibrations between the energies blend together to establish one vibration in harmony.

There are many levels to the depth of blending that can take place with the medium in the altered state of trance. I will try and explain that to you in the next sections, but before I do that, I would like to clear up the misunderstanding that a trance medium cannot hear what is being said through them.

You will often hear trance mediums declaring that, when they are working in an altered state of trance, they are not involved with anything that takes place within the proceedings and that they cannot remember any communication or conversation from the guides and spirit people working through them.

I know from working and developing within the altered state of trance for many years that this statement is incorrect. When working and developing within the altered state, I have found that no matter what depths I would go into within the blending process with my guides and spirit workers, I was always able to hear the tutor's voice controlling the proceedings in the early stages of development.

Now I'm not saying that when you develop into the deeper states of trance blending that you are aware of everything that takes place within the proceedings of the blending process.

There are times within this altered state that you cannot remember everything that has taken place. There are moments of mind blankness that happen within the memory recall.

When you develop into the deeper states, very often you will be aware of the communication that is being spoken through you by the guide or communicator at the time it is being said. It is not until you come out of the blending process that you cannot remember what has been spoken about or discussed but, usually after a short period of time has passed, you will start to recall some of the conversation that had taken place.

If you take the time to research the records of séance with certain pioneers of the past within physical mediumship, then you will find that certain trance mediums were able to hold full conversations while in an altered state through independent voice with their loved ones who were in the spirit side of life at a séance. These mediums were in a deep altered state of trance and their energy fluctuated in and out of the trance state while holding the vibration of the blending energy around them allowing them to speak to their loved ones.

There are certain times within the altered state that a medium will not be able to recall what has happened or what was said through them. Memory loss when in the altered state does happen quite a lot within trance mediumship but not completely all the time. The trance mediums of today are no different to the trance mediums of the past, and the energy of the blending is no different for us as it was in their time.

How Trance Works

The guides and spirit workers who come forward to work through us at the early stages of the blending process do not take complete control over our energy. It is more likely to assume that they will have about 5% control over you at the beginning, which gradually increases over time as you blend with them.

Sitting and blending with your guides and spirit workers eventually allows the percentage to increase in their favour, allowing them to be in more control of the blending process with you. Those working with you will never have complete control over your energy. They may obtain about 95% to 97% but obtaining this level of control with you takes a lot of time and dedication from both sides.

The reason that they will not have 100% control over your energy is that there will always be a small percentage of you involved within the blending process as you are permitting them to blend into your life force energy (your auric field), and they are utilising your physical body as their vessel to work through.

It is important to remember that it is easy for us to interfere with all aspects of trance mediumship in the early stages but, as our understanding and trust deepens, and as they gain more control over our energy, then it becomes harder for us to influence proceedings.

The most important part of development is the intention that we send out to those from spirit who come forward to work with us.

The Light State (Early Stages)

The percentages used in the next sections are only a guideline, and although there are many levels to trance, I have simplified the levels into three sections to make it easier to explain the depth, control and experiences that can take place.

When we first start to sit for the altered states of trance, our minds can become very aware of what is happening around us and we are inclined to interfere with the energy that the spirit people bring forward to us through the blending process. You must allow the energy to gently blend into your auric field and enjoy getting used to the feeling of the process of their energy coming into your energy.

The light state can feel like an overshadowing of their energy taking over our energy when it first starts to come forward. The process of trance blending with your guides and spirit workers never comes forward to us at the front of our bodies. The merging of the two life force energies always begins with the connection being made at the back of our necks, carrying up over our heads and wrapping around our back and shoulders. The energy then travels down the front of our bodies until, eventually, we have the feeling of being completely surrounded inside a bubble of their loving energy.

The blending process can give the feeling that a blanket full of loving energy has been wrapped around you as the merging of the two energies starts to take place. This blanket feeling will allow you to acknowledge the presence of the energy of the spirit person coming forward to blend with you.

This is an important stage in trance development. You must try to focus upon holding this feeling of their energy around you. This allows the merging of the two life force energies to become stronger through time.

You may find that your mind can become active within the process of blending with their energy, and you may only be able to hold their energy in yours for short periods of time as your mind interferes with the process. When this happens and you come out of the blending process, you must go back to the breath and repeat the process of the blending by inviting them back into your energy. The more you blend with them, the stronger the blending will become through time.

Do not try and communicate with them at the early stage when learning to blend with them as your thoughts will interfere with the blending of their energy. On the other hand, if they choose to speak to you then that is different as it is their thoughts that are coming into your mind and not your own thoughts trying to take over within the blending procedure. I would suggest to you that when they speak to you, just listen to what is being said and don't ask them any questions.

Your job as a trance medium is to learn to hold your guides and spirit workers within your energy and we learn to do this through the breath. We do this by allowing the breathing to be as natural as possible. The motion of the breath must be free flowing and must not be laboured as this will interfere with the connection within the blending process.

When we breathe in, we are learning to subconsciously stabilise their energy with our energy and when we exhale, we are relaxing more into the blending.

I'm sure that you will hear at some point on your spiritual journey the old saying that those from the spirit side of life come to us upon the breath. I am inclined to think that what I have just mentioned is what this saying refers to.

This is the reason why breathing exercises are so important for you in your development. The ideal situation is that you will not think about the process of the blending after time but will just naturally go into it through setting your intention at the beginning within the mind and taking that first intake of breath.

When you have sat within the energy of the trance blending for a while, you may start to feel that your throat is starting to swell up or have the feeling that your neck is starting to feel larger as if it is starting to puff up. This is normal progression within your development as those working with you will be looking at developing communication through you.

Our guides and spirit workers do not have a physical voice box or vocal cords, so they have to learn to control our vocal cords through the manipulation of energy when blending with us.

When communication begins to start, it can feel a little strange. You can experience a soft type of growling noise in your throat that you have no control over. You may also experience that your mouth will start to move uncontrollably as they try to take control of the vocal cords.

There may be words that you start to hear within your thoughts in your mind. These words usually start with a "Hello" and then repeats over and over. When the words are heard then they activate your own mind into what is taking place within the blending process and you start to question yourself.

You hear the first "Hello" and then ask yourself, "Did I hear that?" and by the second time you hear the "Hello", you have convinced yourself that it is your own mind taking over and repeating the word and so the battle begins. It truly does become a battle with yourself when the communication starts to come through you.

You will be inclined to hold and swirl the words round about within your mind as you try to decipher if it is spirit or you thinking the words. Doing this can lead to a build-up of energy that can give you an extremely sore head if the words are not released.

Another thing that can take place when holding on to words is an experience of a rush of energy that comes up from your tummy area and into your throat, as you are building up your own confidence to release the word. When this happens, you can start to feel a rush of adrenaline starting from your stomach as you are contemplating saying out loud the word that is repeating in your mind. The rush of energy builds up and then releases and travels up to the throat area as you have eventually convinced yourself in your mind that you are going to release the word this time.

We can feel the word that we have been holding back from releasing resonating through our whole body and, just when it's ready to come out, then we are inclined to swallow the word back down into our tummy and so the process of releasing the word starts again.

What can happen with this surge of energy is that it will keep coming back as before, rushing up from the tummy into the throat area and then, all of a sudden, without warning, it will release with velocity bellowing out through your mouth and into the room. When this occurs, it can totally catch you by surprise as you were unable to swallow the word this time. Then another word will start to form in your mind and the process will start all over again.

Sometimes when the word is released through you with velocity, it can bring you out of the blending process. If this happens, then you just go back into the motion of the breath and re-establish the connection with the guide. The trick is to allow whatever words that come into the mind when sitting in trance to come forward and be heard. It is not our job to try and decipher what is being said.

Building up the confidence to allow the words from your guides or communicators to be spoken freely through you takes a long time with hard work and lots of dedication for all involved. There will be a period of time when the communication that comes through you shall be referred to as the clearing stage. The clearing stage is your thoughts mingling with the thoughts of the spirit people who are working through you. This stage will affect the communication being spoken.

The communication taking place will have some words from spirit and some words from you contained within the conversation. This clearing stage can go on for many months into your development. No-one is exempt from the clearing stage within development.

It is important not to encourage any developing medium who is going through the clearing stage to speak as everything that has been said through them is the true essence of the spirit world. A good tutor will explain what is happening to the developing medium and will guide them to what was said within the communication, clarifying what was the essence of the spirit world and what was the mind of the medium. If this is not corrected at the beginning, then the developing medium can fall into the route of pseudo trance. I will cover this topic in a later section.

Eventually, through time within the blending process, your guide's control becomes stronger with you. When this happens, your mind will become less involved with the conversation that is taking place and the communication will start to become more the essence of the spirit world and with fewer of your own thoughts.

Another experience that can take place as you are blending is the feeling of floating. When you are developing in the light stages, it really is all about you learning to accept the blending process. If you do not sit and blend with them, then your development will not progress.

They must be allowed to come into your energy to change the energy within the vibration created around you.

When sitting in the blending process, you can experience the feeling that your physical body is being stretched upwards, downwards or outwards, and you can also feel that you are being squashed or shrinking within the energy. I have had the feeling of my head being split in two within the energy, when one side of my head felt that it was detached from the other side of my head. These feelings are common within development as those in spirit manipulate the energy around you. This feeling of being stretched within the energy will be with you all through your development, although it does come and go with you through different stages.

The light state is about you learning to trust those who work with you. When they eventually have about 50% control within the blending process, then your development moves onto the next phase. Blending with your guides and spirit workers regularly is the only way for you to advance on to the next stage of your development which I shall call the middle state.

The Middle State

The middle state is the next stage in your development. The procedure of sitting and blending with those who come forward to work with you from the spirit side of life is still the same; that never changes with trance development. What does change is the depth of control that they have over your energy within the vibration created through the blending process.

By now, your mind will have become more settled when you are sitting in the blending process and you will be able to hold their energy within yours for longer. Learning to hold their energy for longer periods of time within your energy is an important part of your development. By doing this, it enables them to have more control over the depth and time that is required to carry out their work through you.

You may start to find, when sitting blending on your own with your guides and spirit workers, that you will become unaware of any thoughts that are in your mind and you may be inclined to think that there is no contact from them. These thoughts can lead to you thinking that you may have fallen asleep when blending with them, but you have not. What is happening is that they are taking your consciousness away from what is taking place within the blending process so they can unfold you deeper into the energy.

Your spirit workers may begin to start holding more one-to-one conversations with you within the blending process. When this happened to me, it would normally take place within the last 15 minutes of sitting with them on my own.

The control of the blending process will become stronger in their favour when sitting with them and you will start to find that there is less interference from you. I have tried on many occasions within this stage of development to deliberately try to interfere with the control of the blend with them, which I found to be a wasted exercise as they knew exactly what I was trying to do and they did not allow it.

You can start to have the sensation within the blending process that your mind is becoming detached from what is taking place within the proceedings. When communication takes place with them, you will hear some of the words that are being spoken but, at this stage within the blending process, you will find that your mind is less involved with the communication that is being spoken through you by them.

Another thing that can happen when you are sitting for communication is that, although you are aware of the words that are being spoken through you, you may find that after the trance sitting, you cannot recall the majority of the conversation that has taken place but, after a few hours, you will start to remember little snippets of the information that was given.

You can also have within the blending process the sensation that you are no longer inside your physical body and can experience that you are standing outside looking at yourself. This phenomenon of your spirit stepping outside your physical body is not confined to any particular stage of the blending process and can happen within all aspects of trance development/ mediumship. I will give a few examples of my own experience with this weird sensation later in the book.

What spirit is striving to achieve with you in the middle state is for them to be able to get more control over your energy within the vibration through the blending process. The control that they are aiming to achieve with you at this stage in your development will eventually be to such a depth that each time you invite them forward to blend into your energy, they will automatically be able to take you to the same depth and level each time. But remember this level of depth takes time to achieve with all concerned.

It is also important to remember that the level of depth that you will be taken to within the blending process is controlled directly by your guides and helpers from the spirit side of life. You cannot take yourself any deeper than what the energy allows within your mediumship.

Although that is not to say that there won't be times in your development that you will try to take yourself deeper into the blending process; however, I can assure you, I have tried many times to take myself deeper into the energy throughout my development and now I understand that the depth of the control within the trance blending is controlled by my spirit team and not by me.

When your guides are able to take you down into the same level of control every time you sit and are able to hold you at that depth each time you blend with them, then the next level in your development is the deeper states.

The middle state is about learning to give more control to your guides from 50% to 90%.

The Deeper State

This deep state is about your guides and spirit workers having about 90% leading to 97% control over your energy within the blending process.

You can only be taken into this deeper level of control under complete guidance and trust between yourself and your spirit team. This level of blending into the altered state takes many years of hard work and dedication to obtain the required depth for them to have a much greater degree of control.

When we talk about the deeper states, what we mean is that there is very little to no interference from the mind of the medium within the blending process. This depth of mediumship is controlled purely through the direction of your guides and spirit workers.

The deeper states are usually associated with physical mediumship and the incredible phenomena that can be generated through the energy created. Although it is nice to experiment with physical mediumship throughout your development, always remember that true controlled physical phenomena cannot be brought forward through your mediumship until your spirit team have complete control over your energy within the trance blending process.

The reason for them to have complete control is that, when we look at developing physical mediumship, the energy created can be harmful to the medium. This can happen if the medium is not developed properly within safe conditions with the right people paying attention and taking care with the proceedings that are unfolding.

We are dealing with an energy that we know from the teachings of pioneers of the past can be harmful to the medium if certain guidelines and safety precautions are not adhered to by all involved.

When you are sitting for development in the deep state, it is advisable that you make sure that all phones (mobile and landline) are switched off or on flight mode and your doorbell is turned off. The reason for this is that any noise carries a vibration and, when in this deeper state, the vibration created is amplified, and because your senses are heightened, any unexpected noise can send shock waves through your body. Your spirit team must be able to control the energy in their favour to protect you.

When working and developing within the energy blending of the altered state, certain changes can start to happen with how you feel within your own energy. In the earlier stages of development when your awareness returns back after you have been sitting and blending with your guides, you can feel completely energised, full of life and refreshed.

The deeper states can have a totally opposite effect upon your energy. I now find that after sitting and blending in the deeper states, I can feel exhausted and can take anything up to 30 minutes before I feel back to normal.

All development into the altered states of trance is about learning to create a purer connection with those who come forward from the spirit side of life to blend into your energy. Through time, your guides will be able to hold you for longer periods within the deeper state, then you will have a greater understanding of the control within the blending of the trance energy.

You should now be able to go into the same depth of trance blending each time you sit with your guides and spirit workers, without having to give any concern about the connection that is being made with you, through the blending process with them.

You will have now realised within your trance mediumship, that the depths that can be achieved through the blending process are controlled by them, and your job is just to be the best vessel for them to use and for you to accept, without question, the energy of the blending that can be obtained with them.

Unlike the early stages of trance development when you are inclined to interfere with the blending process by bringing your thoughts into the proceedings, when you have reached the deeper state, you will know beyond doubt if the energy of the blending with your spirit workers feels deep or light to you.

The reason for this is that by this stage, you will have the understanding within your own mediumship that you will work in the depth of energy that the guide or helper from the spirit side of life wishes to work in. Some guides will bring forward a very light energy to you and some will like to work in a heavier energy. Your job is to go with what feels right to you but to accept that they are in control in all times in the depth of the energy of the blending.

Deeper Trance Communication

When communication takes place within a one-to-one trance reading, the medium's awareness is pushed to one side, allowing either the guide to relay the message on behalf of the loved one in spirit or the loved one can come forward and blend into the energy of the medium and speak directly to the person receiving the information.

When communication happens in the deeper states, it must be able to take place under the direct control of your guides and members of your spirit team. The guides must have control over the blending of the energy, so that they are able to freely explain to the group what they intend to do.

The deeper state allows direct communication without the mind of the medium becoming involved in the proceedings. It has been documented that in deep state communication, foreign languages have been spoken through various mediums when in the altered state. These mediums have no knowledge of these foreign languages and it proves the existence of a superior knowledge working through them. Always remember that you are only the vessel for them to utilise and administrate the information through.

Another thing that can take place when in an altered state is that you can have the feeling that the energy of the blending is fluctuating in and out. This can happen all through your development but, by now, with your gained understanding of the trance energy within the blending process, you will not interfere with it and simply trust.

An Observation With Fluctuation Of The Energy

We often talk about the pioneers of the past and the wonderful achievements that the spirit world has shown us through the mediumship of physical phenomena. Those mediums who had the correct chemical composition within their energy to produce what is required for physical mediumship have always been very rare within the spiritual community and we make reference to them as being deep trance mediums.

I'm a great believer in people paying attention to what they read and when listening to conversations that take place within the spiritual community with trance mediums of today.

I touched upon earlier that many trance mediums often lay claim that they have no recollection of any conversation that has taken place within the deeper states of trance communication. This is a rare occurrence, and I am not saying it can't happen after some trance demonstrations or readings, but the majority of trance mediums will remember little aspects of the proceedings that have taken place. They may not remember anything immediately after the event but, as time unfolds, they will remember little pieces of the communication that had taken place as their own energy settles back around them.

I found it interesting, when researching trance mediumship within my own spiritual journey, that lots of books I came across were written about the pioneers of the past. If you take the time to read between the lines within some of these books, you will find that when physical demonstrations were taking place in séance conditions, it is clearly noted that when the phenomenon of independent voice was being produced and demonstrated some of the mediums who were demonstrating this rare type of mediumship were able to hold one-to-one conversations with their loved ones in spirit whilst being in the deep state of blending. These amazing occurrences of holding conversations with their loved ones actually took place without any interference from the medium within the connection of the energy producing the phenomena.

I can only surmise that the understanding and trust that these mediums had with their guides had developed to such a deep level of control that the trance energy they were connected into was at such a depth that, when the energy fluctuated during the blending with the medium, the medium's spirit team were able to hold the energy without the thoughts of the medium interfering with what was taking place.

Pseudo Trance

The problem that arises with pseudo trance is not usually within the blending process, if the developing trance medium has been taught correctly to enable their guides and helpers to blend correctly into their energy.

Pseudo trance happens when the medium's mind subconsciously takes control over the blending process and pushes the spirit people away, leaving them to believe that the connection is still there with their guides and helpers.

The problem arises when they go to demonstrate their trance mediumship through communication or healing. You will often find that the medium does not realise that they have interfered within the blending of the energies between themselves and their spirit workers and strongly believe that the communication being spoken through them or the healing taking place is conducted by their spirit team.

It is important to understand that there is a very fine line between us interfering with the thoughts of our spirit guides and our own thoughts within the blending process.

One of the reasons causing interference to take place with the developing trance medium is that the people who are sitting for the development of the medium are themselves unsure of the workings of the altered states of trance. This can mean they confuse the thoughts coming from the medium's own mind with the words of the guides and workers from the spirit world.

This can, if not corrected quickly, lead to the medium taking complete control over the communication that is taking place and will end up having no essence whatsoever of the teachings or wisdom from the spirit world.

This can also take place within trance healing as the medium's mind takes control over the blending process with the healing guide and interferes with the proceedings.

The simple thought of the medium starting to think that they are the healer and not the healing vessel can push the healing guides' energy out of their energy and change the dynamics from trance energy to magnetic healing.

I suppose another problem that can arise with pseudo trance is that the medium is not willing to put the time and hard effort into the development of trance and, although they may well understand the mechanics of it, without the time spent blending with their guides, they will never truly understand the connection that is made between the two energies through the blending process.

There is a great demand for people to experience and witness trance in its truest form and many people who witness demonstrations do not truly understand it. It is important to listen to the content of what is being said through the trance medium and not to be taken in by a voice that may sound completely different to the medium's.

When you are witnessing the true essence of spirit communication, the connection to the energy of the spirit world will draw you to the edge of your seat. You will be captivated with every word that comes forward through the love of the connection to the energy created.

If you find yourself starting to fidget or looking around the room and the communication that is taking place is not holding your attention, then you are not witnessing the true essence of the love of the spirit world but the thoughts and words of a medium in pseudo trance.

Educate yourself by trusting your gut feeling. Learn to listen to the content of what is being said through the medium on behalf of the spirit world. Think about it. Does it resonate with you or confuse you? The most important thing I can say to you is... trust your own intuition.

Trance Recoveries

This area of trance work is something that requires a special kind of medium to practise it. This mediumship work is not for everyone although, saying that, these types of séances are utilised by the spirit world to help lost spirit people connect back into the love of heaven.

In my own experience, the energy that came forward when working with this type of mediumship had the feeling of being heavy, dense and very negative. I will give you a couple of examples from my observations with this type of work.

I was at a trance development group and had the pleasure of

watching a lady in the séance cabinet bringing forward a person from the spirit side of life. The lady went quiet and was just sitting in the cabinet when, all of a sudden, the energy within the room started to change. The energy started to become heavier, creating an eerie feeling.

I remember having a good look about the room when, to my great surprise, I became aware of a thick mist appearing that was coming down from the top of the door which was behind me and was slowly creeping along the floor towards the direction of the séance cabinet. It was like watching an old vampire film from years ago from the Hammer House of Horror. It felt unsettling.

The lady medium who was sitting in the cabinet started to ask: "Where am I?" She kept on repeating the same question over and over. The circle leader started to ask her questions and the lady in the cabinet started to become upset. I just listened and watched as the events unfolded.

The circle leader explained to the group that what was taking place with the lady in the cabinet was a spirit recovery and she was going to help put the spirit person into the light. The circle leader was speaking to the spirit person who had blended with the medium and asked if they were able to see a light.

She repeated the question until eventually the spirit person with the medium answered, "Yes!" The tutor then asked, "Can you see a guide or a person standing at the light?" "Yes!" was shouted out through the medium. Then the tutor asked for the spirit person to head towards the light.

There seemed to be a bit of hesitation from the spirit person to head towards the light. Once guidance and reassurance were given that everything would be well and that their friends and family were there to receive them, the spirit person headed towards the light and said that they could see their loved ones waiting for them. The tutor asked the spirit person to continue into the light and be at peace. After a few minutes of silence, the tutor explained to the group that the spirit person was now in the light.

The circle leader then asked the medium to slowly return her conscious mind back into the room. I watched as the medium slowly returned back to herself and the thick mist within the séance room disappeared. I was fascinated with everything that had taken place. I had never been involved in a trance spirit recovery.

I was sitting with the same group a few months later and was having my turn sitting in the séance cabinet with a red light in front of me when a blending of energy came over me that felt as if, all of a sudden, I had become childlike. I heard a little trembling voice that spoke through me saying, "Where is my mummy? I want my mummy." I could feel the anguish of the little child as she kept asking for her mother.

The little girl became very upset and started to sob uncontrollably. I could feel her pain and confusion and started to cry along with her. The more the little girl got upset, the more I got upset. I could not stop crying. I could feel my whole body trembling with the emotion that was taking place. The little girl said through the tears that she was in hospital and had closed her eyes and, when she opened them, she could not find her mummy.

I heard the circle leader saying to the little girl, "Can you see anyone around you who you know?" The little girl replied that she could see no-one. I asked within my mind for my guides to intervene and help this little girl, in between me shaking like a leaf and crying uncontrollably.

I became aware of a white light appearing in my mind and Henry standing alongside an elderly lady. The circle leader then asked if she could see a white light and the little girl said through me, "Yes." "Please walk towards the white light," the circle leader said to her. The little girl then replied, "I can see my granny!" and her tears and emotions heightened. I was aware of Henry reuniting the little girl with her granny and taking her into the light.

The energy of the blending started to dissipate and I started to come out of the altered state. When I had fully returned, I was in pieces. My emotions were all over the place, I could not stop crying. I was exhausted and completely drained of all energy.

I spoke to Henry about it a few days later and he told me that this type of mediumship was not for everyone and they would only bring people forward to me for this type of work under their direction and I was not to sit for development for trance recoveries.

I have decided to leave this type of work to those who have chosen to develop this aspect of mediumship. There are specific trance group circles whose primary aim is to develop this particular avenue of assisting lost souls.

Although I found it very interesting and the energy completely different within this work, I have always taken Henry's advice and I do not directly sit for trance recoveries, but I do not have a problem with them if they are brought forward by my spirit team.

Developing On Your Own

This is a subject that differs between mediums. Some are inclined to say that development takes place in classes, and this is true to some degree, and others will have the opinion that it will be blending on your own with your guides that develops you.

When you join a class for any type of mediumship, you will normally find that the development is structured with exercises to help you establish a link to the spirit world. You will find that the exercises are usually tried and tested, and are a good way to develop in a safe environment. You will hear from some mediums that you need to develop in a group because of the energy that is created within the circle.

I found on my own journey that this was not the case; although I enjoyed my trance development groups and attended them regularly, the bulk of my trance development has taken place when sitting blending with my guides on my own.

The groups were a good foundation for me to build up trust with my spirit team as being in the trance circle with others gave me the opportunity to feel safe, until the time came that I was confident enough to sit with spirit on my own. Being in a trance circle also gave me the opportunity to discuss within the group what I had felt and experienced within the blending process.

When I had the confidence within myself to sit with spirit on my own, then I would sit and blend with my guides and helpers five days a week and have the weekend off, unless I was attending a trance workshop.

I first started to sit and blend daily with spirit for about 30 minutes each time, gradually building up over a period of time to one and a half hours every day. I always made sure that the room where I was sitting and blending with spirit was always quite dark, although sitting in the dark is not required for trance. I would listen to a recording of raindrops hitting onto a tin roof. I found that the repetitive sound helped me to block out all my other thoughts as I learned to discipline my mind and sit in the stillness.

Learning to still the mind takes time and hard work. I would sit and wait for the loving feeling of the blending taking place with my guides as their life force came forward and blended into my energy. It would feel like a blanket of love had been wrapped around my body, a warm secure feeling that always just felt right.

I would often find myself just sitting basking in the energy of trance as if I was bathing in an energy of love, just enjoying what was taking place with no expectations. When sitting blending, I started to become aware of colours that filled my mind and I would often find myself chasing the shapes of the colours within my eyelids that were firmly closed.

The energy within the blending started to feel that it was becoming stronger the more I sat with my guides. I would have the sensation of beginning to float within the colour, it was as if motion and time had stopped around me and I was just becoming one with the swirling colour. My mind would feel as if it was starting to become detached from my physical body. I would no longer be aware of sitting in the room and it felt wonderful.

The more I sat blending with them, the more my mind was becoming detached from the proceedings, eventually to the extent that I would feel the energy of the blending take hold of me and then I could not remember anything else that had taken place. At first, I thought I had fallen asleep within the energy as this would explain why I would have no recollection of where I had been or how long I had sat for.

This experience of not knowing where my conscious mind has been taken to when blending on my own with my guides still takes place today after sitting and developing with them for many years. I do understand that you can fall asleep when sitting but it is quite rare. The energy of the spirit world is alive, it is vibrant and those who live in that dimension do not sleep.

The reason for them taking your consciousness away from what is happening is that they are developing your mediumship through the blending of energy and it is easier for them to do this without our thoughts interfering with what is taking place.

Another thing that can happen when sitting in the altered state is that, all of a sudden, one or both of your arms can rise up and slam down at an alarming rate bringing you out of the blending with a jolt to the physical body.

I don't know why this happens. I have asked many times and always got the reply that it can happen. So please remember that if you are jolted out of the blending process, you may become disoriented, have the feeling of nausea and the sensation of being out of sorts within your own general well-being.

These sensations are not only associated with you experiencing a jolt while sitting, they can also take place if you happen to bring yourself out of the blending process too quickly. So always remember, if you experience any of these sensations, take my advice on board: go back into the blending process and allow the energy to settle around you before bringing your consciousness back into the room.

I have heard mediums saying that when sitting blending on their own, they have set up recording devices just in case the spirit people blending with them want to relay some guidance to them when developing. In my opinion, I do not think this is a good idea. It may work for some people but I would be inclined to think that, if this device was set up, then the mind and the desires of the medium could influence what was being said. I think it is better to just let your development unfold naturally through hard work under the direction and control of your guides.

The blending process is how they develop you as a trance

medium and the energy they bring will change your emotions for the better through the love they bring to you.

Emotions

Emotions are something that we are inclined to try to hide from people but you can't hide them from yourself or from your spirit guides when you are allowing their energy to come into your energy.

We all like to think that we are in control of our emotions and we can keep them in check but I'm not afraid to say that when you are allowing the love of the spirit world to draw close to you, then your emotions become heightened and harder to deal with.

These changes that occur within you do not happen overnight, they seem to creep up on you gradually over a period of time and, before you know it, the slightest thing can set you off.

You will find that you become more sympathetic towards others and can feel the hurt and sadness that emanates from them through the energy that they are carrying within their auric field.

You can find that the littlest of things can start you off with floods of tears that would never have affected you before embarking on your spiritual journey. I have always tried to suppress my emotions in everything I did and thought I had become good at not showing my tears, anger or frustration to anyone outside my immediate family circle. I always thought of myself as a man's man and certain things I would hide from people around me.

Things started to change one evening while sitting watching a movie. I suppose this was the trigger point for me to experience the changes taking place within my emotions. The film came to a sad part and, all of a sudden, tears started streaming down my face. I had no control over this emotion and found myself asking what the hell was wrong with me.

Another time, I was sitting unwinding after holding a healing clinic and thinking about the clients who had come through the door that day. This led to me having a tearful moment on my own. I realised that the tears coming forward were for the love of the clients who I had worked with and, after listening to their concerns, their emotions within their energy had touched my emotions and pulled upon my heartstrings without me realising it.

One day I received some sad news that a client who I had got very close to had passed over to the world of spirit and, to be honest, this news made me angry inside. Instead of feeling sad, I couldn't stop venting my frustration to my spirit team which was totally out of character for me.

These are just a few experiences of my emotions being turned upside down through development with my spirit team. These mixed feelings repeatedly keep coming forward into my life because of my development. It is something I have had to come to accept but it was not something I was used to experiencing. It did take me quite a long time to get to grips with the highs and lows of my emotional energy.

I do not hide from my emotions anymore. They are part of who I have become today. The change that has been made makes me a more compassionate and considerate person towards others and the situations that can take place within our lives.

These emotions have also helped with my own understanding that I am more able to relate to people's feelings through my own heightened emotions, which enable me to have more of an understanding and desire to help those in need.

When we participate in retreats or workshops and are working in the energy of the spirit world, our energy and emotions become heightened. We can have real feelings of intense emotion that take place within our own energy. These feelings can stay with us all through the duration of the events that we are taking part in. They can even continue to stay with us for a few days after the event has concluded.

What can happen a few days later, when you are out of the energy, is that your emotions can change from the feeling of being in a high state of consciousness to the feeling of a change in your mood and well-being becoming very low. It can feel as if there is a slight depression coming over you as your energy level drops from the high to the low. This is a common occurrence that you may well experience after you have been working in the energy within the altered states of trance over a period of a few days.

If you experience this change in your mood and energy, then please note that your energy levels will start to settle back after a day or two, bringing your emotions back into line, allowing you to start feeling balanced again.

Itchy Sensation

When you are learning to hold the energy of those from the spirit side of life within your own energy through the blending process, you can experience a sensation of spirit energy that can feel like you have lice in your hair or cobwebs that are building up over your face.

Some people find that their skin becomes itchy all over their body. This feeling can be mild for some and for others the feeling of the itchiness can be unbearable. This itchy feeling does not last with you forever in your development but can come back from time to time depending on what type of mediumship you are looking to develop.

When you experience this energy, you must try not to scratch yourself. If you do scratch, then you can bring yourself out of the blending process. You have to learn to work through it, no matter how much it irritates you. Ask your guides to calm down the itching; it will take time but eventually the itching subsides.

The reason why the itching takes place is because those who are coming forward to blend with you are bringing their energy into your energy which starts to vibrate into your vibration generating the feeling of the energy crawling over your physical body.

This feeling of the energy crawling over your hair and body is not just felt by individual people sitting for trance development; there can be instances when the energy can be generated in a room and it can be felt by a group of people at the same time. The group could be watching a demonstration or sitting for a medium for physical development in séance conditions.

In my development, I went through a period of going into the blending process for about six weeks where the blending of the energy felt very light. The lightness of the blending did not give me concern although I had not felt it this light for many years. I just accepted the depth of the energy that was with me and settled into the development that was taking place.

During this time, I started to feel an energy that tickled on an area of my forehead. The energy tickled at my third eye area constantly and never halted for a minute every time I sat within the blending process. The tickling drove me mad, it never halted, but I persevered with it.

I was constantly asking my guides to stop it but they never did. I trusted that there was a reason for it, although I never found out what it was from them or why it had taken place.

I suppose they were developing my third eye for future work but, on the other side of the coin, I often wonder if they were testing me to see if I would give up but I never did.

Facial Overshadowing

Spirit facial overshadowing within our energy is a wonderful experience for those sitting observing the proceedings.

The spirit people are able to bring their energy into our energy and create an image that is very similar to a holographic image that is generated over the physical face and sometimes the body of the medium.

They are able to generate these phenomena at a rapid speed over the medium's face and you can be aware of lots of different people from the spirit side of life showing themselves one after the other at an astonishing rate.

Through this ability, they are also able to bring the image of your loved ones to you which truly is a wonderful experience for you and them, especially when you recognise them.

The energy eventually starts to become stronger around the medium as the guides take more control over the proceedings. This allows them to make the energy stronger enabling them to settle the vibration around the medium as they show themselves more clearly to the group.

When this takes place, they are able to hold their image for longer periods of time within the holographic-type image, sometimes even when they are communicating through the medium. Please remember that this type of phenomena is not to be confused as transfiguration.

Transfiguration is a totally different type of phenomenon that is generated through the energy created by a physical medium.

Transfiguration

Transfiguration is a wonderful phenomenon to witness. It is a wonderful thing to see the development of it taking place with a physical medium.

Transfiguration can only be shown through a medium who has the quality within their chemical make-up that makes them a physical medium. The medium must possess a particular genetic and physical characteristic within their energy that is needed by spirit to manifest this type of phenomena.

This type of mediumship is as rare today as it was a hundred years ago, and I am afraid to say that not everyone who develops to be a trance medium will have the quality within their energy to develop physical mediumship.

Transfiguration is controlled by the spirit people working

with the medium by enabling them to create an ectoplasmic-type structure that we make reference to as a "mask" within the energy from the spirit world and the medium's energy.

The energy structure starts to build up in front of the medium's face which can look like a blurry mass. This energy becomes stronger and the appearance of the medium's head becomes mannequin-looking. There are no features that can be seen on the medium's face as the energy that has been built up in front of the medium distorts it.

The ectoplasmic mask then forms in front of the medium's face about one to two inches away from the physical head. It does not attach directly onto the medium's face, there is always a slight gap. Then what takes place truly is a phenomenon. The spirit person coming forward, which is usually a guide at first, pushes their life force energy into the ectoplasmic mask.

When they do this, the mask forms to their energy shape, creating their image to form a physical likeness in front of the medium's head within the formed mask. The image will then retract back into the mass of energy allowing other spirit people to come forward to repeat the same procedure over and over.

When the spirit people are showing themselves through the blending with the mask, there will be no direct communication taking place through the medium. The energy that has been built up to show these phenomena needs to be strong and focused, and communication requires a shift within the energy that will change the vibration and dissipate the ectoplasmic mask. They can, however, hear you and can acknowledge questions put forward to them with a nod of the medium's head.

There can be times while people are observing transfiguration when they will recognise their loved ones from spirit showing themselves within the structure of the mask. When this happens, it is important to acknowledge them as the contact created through the vibration of your voice can help to make the image stronger.

There may be the opportunity, if beckoned by the medium under the control of the spirit person working through them, to be able to touch the hand of their loved one from spirit.

This works by the medium, under the direction of the spirit person, putting out their physical hand and the person who recognised their loved one is directed to come forward and place their hand outwards and wait for their loved one controlling the medium to touch their hand.

However, you must not put your physical hand into the vibration of the energy within the séance cabinet or try to grab the hand of the medium who is in the altered state of your own accord. This action can be harmful to the medium and everything that takes place within the manifestation of the transfiguration must be under the direction and control of the spirit world at all times.

Spirit Children

Spirit children are cherished and adored in the world of spirit because of the purity and innocence that they carry within their energy.

They are involved in many aspects of our mediumship and are only allowed to venture into our physical environment through the protection and guidance of the people from the spirit side of life who look after them.

Many children who live in the world of spirit can decide if they wish to remain as children and others can decide to grow into adulthood, it is a personal choice.

When a parent loses a child, it can be a devastating time in their lives but it is comforting to know that they will never lose the bond of love that is formed with that child. The parents only lose the physical contact for a period of time and will be reunited back together with their loved one when they return home to the spirit realm.

I would like to tell you about a lady who came to visit one of my healing clinics who was with child and explained that she had been informed by the specialists in the hospital that there were complications with the child within the womb.

It saddens me to say that the child did not survive onto the earth plane and returned back home to the world of spirit, but the understanding that was sought through this tragic event was of great help to both the parents and me.

I never normally work with anyone who is with child unless they have had devastating news about the child and that the outcome of the prognosis from the specialist is understood.

The lady arrived at my clinic after attending many hospital appointments and had been given the news that all parents dread, that the child, in the specialist's opinion, was not going to survive.

My heart went out to the lady the more she described her situation to me. I explained to the lady that I never promise to be able to cure any condition or ailment with anyone who seeks help from the spirit world. I am only the vessel for my spirit team to utilise as a channel enabling them to come forward and see what they can do to help.

The lady agreed with what had been discussed with her and proceeded to go ahead with the healing. As she lay upon the healing bed, I set my intentions for a healing to take place with my spirit team and blended into the altered state of trance.

I remember putting my hands above the area of her womb and could feel immense energy transmitting through my hands into that area. This lasted for quite some time and then I became aware of my guide speaking to me. The guide was explaining that the child was going to return back to the world of spirit and it was never the agreement for the child to be born onto the material world.

The guide proceeded to explain more information to me which, in due course, I later explained to the mother. I will share this with you now:

I gently broke the news to the lady that the spirit of her child had made an agreement to be placed into her womb with the intention of not being born into our side of life. When a new spirit is placed into the womb, there is automatically a bond of love that can never be separated from a parent and a child. The spirit child will always know their parents and the parents will always know the energy and vibration created by their own child.

There is never sadness from the spirit people when knowing that the baby will not be born into the material side of life. The sadness that is felt on the material world is through the parents and other family members who have to come to terms with the grief of losing a child.

The reason the new spirit agrees to this decision not to be born into our world is that the energy created within spirit children is needed on the spirit side of life. The innocence contained in the love of a spirit child carries a purity of light transmitting within their energy that is utilised and absorbed within the energy of the spirit realms.

The mother may feel from time to time, when carrying the child in the womb, a feeling of emptiness, as if the child is not there anymore. This happens when the spirit child is connecting back into the energy of the spirit world, getting themselves ready to return back home. The spirit child will not return home until they know that the parents are ready to accept the inevitable, however hard the situation may be.

It saddens me to say that this turn of events had happened to this lady on more than one occasion in her life but the explanation given to her by me through my guide, however hard for her to accept, hopefully gave her a better understanding and enabled her to take the positives from the negatives.

It is comforting to know that all children are cherished in the spirit world. It is also comforting to know that any child who is taken from us, from the physical world or from the womb, will automatically be collected by a loved one on the spirit side of life.

A child who has never touched upon the earth plane can make the same choices as a child who has sadly been taken from the physical world. They have unconditional free will allowing them to choose what they would like to do. All children in the world of spirit will come around about their parents regularly for a visit.

I would like to think that, when this happens, an angel has been created and released back into the spirit world.

Spirit Children Activity

It is always a privilege to become aware of children's energy within your mediumistic journey. The energy that is created by them is always a loving energy and always seems to bring comfort to myself and the person who they are attached to.

My first experience of becoming aware of a child from spirit who was attached to someone was when I was giving a reading at a development group for platform mediumship.

I was paired up with a lady to practise giving over information received from spirit. I was new to this and I was a little bit scared of telling her what I had received. The information was coming forward and, after about five minutes of giving over whatever was coming into my mind, I became aware of a little girl who slowly appeared by poking her head around the side of the lady as if the little girl was playing peekaboo.

I could see the little girl's face so clearly and explained to the lady that this little girl was appearing and disappearing to the side of her. The lady asked me to describe the little girl to her. I gave the description of what I was seeing and it turned out that the little girl was her daughter who had sadly passed to the world of spirit about a year previously. The confirmation that her daughter was still around her and very much part of her life brought tears of happiness to her.

I often see little spirit children around people when working with them within the altered states. I find it comforting to think that when we are devastated by the loss of a child that the child is regularly around the parents.

I was holding a healing clinic and working with a client in Peterhead. The client fell asleep upon the therapy bed while the healing was taking place. I had finished the healing when, to my surprise, I saw a pair of little hands come up from the side of the bed followed by the most beautiful little girl's face with blonde curly locks. Then another little set of hands appeared alongside the little girl's and another set of hands alongside the second set of hands.

Then, all of a sudden, I was looking at three gorgeous little children at different ages. One was the little girl and the other two were little boys who were peering over the side of the bed staring at the gentleman lying upon the bed. I heard a tiny voice saying: "That's my daddy!" and "That's my mummy!"

I could hardly believe my eyes! I started up a conversation with the lady who had come in with the gentleman. I gently managed to shift the conversation round to asking if she had lost any children into the world of spirit. She said that she had lost three children over a few years. I gently explained to her that I had become aware of them being with her and that they had appeared to me within the healing room, so I could let her know they were around her and her husband.

The turn of events that had taken place that day truly was a privilege for me. I was so happy that the children had appeared right in front of my eyes and that they had shown themselves in such a fashion that I was able to confirm with their mother that they were around.

Another time when spirit children are present is when a séance is taking place. Many spirit children who come along to a séance are usually attached to a loved one within the group but there are a few who are there just to help with the uplifting of the energy.

These spirit children help with many aspects of what takes place within the proceedings of the séance. They can help to move items within the room especially toys that have been laid out for them to play with. They can gently pull at people's hair and delicately stroke them allowing the sitters to feel the loving touch of the spirit.

They can help build up and manipulate the energy needed in a physical séance by dancing, skipping and running around the room. When a demonstration of table tipping is underway, you can usually see little spirit children's hands in between the gaps of the hands of the people around the table.

You can also feel and see the energy of the children around the séance trumpets as they try to attach and manipulate the trumpets to move. Children are always present within the proceedings of a physical séance but they will never be introduced by the spirit world into any situation unless they are in a completely safe environment.

I was at a week-long trance workshop held in Wales and, in the evening, we were sitting watching other members of the group going into the séance cabinet. One of the mediums who went into the cabinet that night went into a deep state and we started to smell a strange odour in the room that turned out to be related to ectoplasm.

This was the first time that I had ever smelt the substance of ectoplasm, and for those who ask what it smells like, I will try my best to explain it for you. The smell that filled the room that evening from the direction of the séance cabinet was like a pungent smell of bleach that had been lying on a damp cloth, mixed with sulphur and rotten eggs. We did not witness any ectoplasm materialise with the medium that evening but to smell it was a privilege.

What happened next was amazing! As I focused on the odour that was in the room, I became aware of lots of spirit children who appeared within the circle. I felt the energy of a little girl who stopped in front of me and she said, "Hello! I'm Annabella but you can call me Bella." "Hello!" I said in disbelief at what I was experiencing. Then the little girl said, "I'm going to play now," and she started to skip away and join in with the other little spirit children who were dancing and running around within the circle.

The memory of what took place that evening had never left me and it wasn't until a few years later that it all fell into place. I was sitting one evening in my own group for physical development, when I became aware of a beautiful little girl who was a regular visitor to the group.

The little girl is called Bella and is attached to her mother, who is a developing medium within the group. That evening little Bella had decided to talk directly to me and she said, "I'm called Annabella but you can call me Bella."

I had never made the connection! I had sat with the mother

of little Bella for many years and would never have guessed in a month of Sundays that little Bella who first came to speak to me in Wales was the same little girl.

This beautiful little spirit girl had known that her mother was going to be developing trance mediumship long before I had ever met her mother and she had taken the time to introduce herself.

Spirit children carry an energy of pure love and innocence and sometimes a vibration full of mischief that can be felt by all when their energy is introduced into the room.

To give an example, I can often misplace my keys amongst other small items in my home. I usually turn my house upside down searching for the said item and, when I'm at a complete loss, then the said item usually appears, as if by magic, on top of the table, worktop or on the arm of my couch in plain view to the world.

I know from experience that my little spirit helper, Chuckles, has a hand in the moving of these items within my home. I've grown accustomed to it over the years and just ask him to return the items. I'm sure that he gets great pleasure in seeing me running around like a headless chicken searching!

Spirit Helpers

This is a subject that I suppose we are inclined to overlook.

We often only think about guides and communicators who work through us and never really give much thought about the other jobs that those who live in the spirit world have chosen to do.

There is one particular turn of events that changed my perception of what they do from spirit which involved my daughter. My daughter had been out for an evening with friends and one of her party fell onto a bottle and cut her wrist so severely that the girl ended up in accident and emergency.

When my daughter was in the waiting area in the hospital, she became aware of a young man from spirit standing alongside her. The young man never spoke to her. When she returned to her own home after her friend had been discharged from hospital, the young man from spirit arrived at her home.

I received a phone call from my daughter the following morning telling me what had happened with her friend, and about the young man she had become aware of in the hospital and how he had arrived back at her home.

My daughter was concerned for the young man as she was unsure if he had passed over within the hospital and was now lost or stuck in that environment. She asked if it was at all possible that I could ask my guides to go and have a look to find out if the young man was OK.

I spoke to Henry about it and he said, "Give me a few minutes and I will go and find out what has taken place." A few minutes later I heard Henry's voice saying, "I have spoken to the young man." I immediately asked what had happened and was given an explanation that I was not expecting.

Henry went on to say that the young man's job was to look after those who bring in people who seek medical help to bring love and comfort to them as they are usually upset with the uncertainty of bringing loved ones or friends when visiting a hospital environment. The young man knew that my daughter was aware of him and his own curiosity had brought him to travel back with my daughter to her home.

Henry continued, "He is not supposed to travel away from the hospital environment and has been spoken to about what his job entails. He won't be back visiting your daughter at her home."

I passed this information on to my daughter which made her mind more at ease but the turn of events started my own mind thinking about the jobs that people can choose to do when in the world of spirit.

I know that there are spirit healers, doctors, surgeons and nurses who help in hospital environments along with other spirit people who choose to collect those who go through into the transition of life, but I never gave any thought to spirit workers like this young man who was there helping with the emotions of friends and family members attending the hospital.

I used to think that when people became aware of spirit people wandering around within the hospital they were witnessing people who had just passed over or were seeing spirit people attached to the people in the hospital.

Those who live in the spirit world have a variety of jobs that they do but we never really give a second thought to what they are. We tend to get caught up in our own mediumship with our own guides and helpers and then only start to think about the other jobs that spirit workers do when something takes place to activate our thoughts.

We know that there are people in spirit who come forward to hear and collect our healing requests and prayers, and then they take the information back to their side of life and distribute them like a postal service to the appropriate people to act upon the request.

There are people who organise our loved ones in spirit to let them know that their family members and friends on our side of life will be attending a séance or a demonstration of mediumship.

Some spirit people have the job of collecting people who return back to the spirit side of life. Now we know that when this takes place, it is usually family members who are there to meet and greet them, but in certain times, like war for instance, when mass death takes place, then other spirit people take on the job of retrieving those who have transitioned into the heavenly world.

There are people who take on the job of counselling people when they have entered into the world of spirit. When children return back to spirit, there are people who dedicate their lives to nourishing and looking after them as they grow into adults.

There are many people who dedicate their lives to inventing things in the spirit world to help humanity. The list of what people on the spirit side of life do to help is endless.

I could go on all day listing their jobs but I hope that the few who I have touched upon will give you a better understanding that those in the spirit world all work together doing all that they can to help us.

Teaching The Altered State Of Trance

Teaching was something that I never gave much thought to. I was so focused upon my own development and trying to be the best vessel for my own team to work through that it never crossed my mind.

I had attended many trance workshops over the years and I enjoyed every one of them, although I must confess some of the teachings I received left me a little confused at times within my journey for trance development. I quickly learned to absorb the teachings and advice which resonated within me and to disregard what did not from the tutors at the workshops.

The job of a tutor is to help guide you on your spiritual journey; to give you reassurance and encouragement on behalf of the spirit world that what you are experiencing within your mediumship is to be expected and all part of your development.

The tutor must be able to observe the connection that is being made with an understanding of what is taking place within the energy, and be able to listen and communicate with the spirit world and reiterate the guidance that they are receiving from them to help you with your development.

The tutor will take you through exercises that will enable you to connect properly into the vibrational energy of your guides from the spirit world, and should always be true to themselves and their students when the connection is not correct or that particular type of mediumship is not for them or not for them at this particular stage of their development.

The tutor cannot and does not develop your energy for mediumship. That side of your development regarding the energy changes within and around you is controlled and developed from the spirit side of life with the help of your guides and spirit workers blending into your energy.

They do this by bringing their energy into your auric field

which is your life force energy. This is done through the connection of the two energies merging together through the blending process which is controlled by your guides and spirit workers who work with and alongside you in your development.

I had been working within the altered state of trance mediumship for quite a few years and I was running healing clinics and closed groups for trance development. I had been receiving lots of enquiries from people wanting to know how to develop trance mediumship and trance healing. I always got back to them and promised that I would get round to looking into organising workshops and events but I always seemed to talk myself out of doing anything.

Then one day, when sitting blending in the trance energy on my own, I had a conversation with Henry and he asked that I start to look at teaching the development of trance and trance healing.

I'm delighted that the conversation took place with Henry as it has brought a greater understanding of trance development to me and a different approach to the workings of individuals and how spirit work with each person. I have always tried to keep my approach to development the same as Henry's approach to mediumship and healing by keeping it: SIMPLE!

The blending of spirit energy with our own energy is, and always should be, a natural occurrence within your mediumship. The hardest part for them is not the blending process but us learning to hold them within our energy through the breath. The breath must be natural and not laboured. Having a laboured breath makes the energy of the blend jerky and pushes their energy backwards away from you.

In your mind, try to adopt the thought as you breathe in, when the blending is taking place, that you are pulling their energy closer into your energy and when you exhale you are relaxing and stabilising the process of the two energies becoming one. Through time you will never give a second thought to the breathing process as it will be lodged into your subconscious mind.

Through helping people to develop trance mediumship, I have had the pleasure of experiencing some of the most wonderful things that take place within the workings of the spirit world and have truly witnessed some of the strangest things around people while they have been blended with spirit that I would like to share with you.

I was at a workshop, with about 16 people attending, when I became aware of a build-up of energy around the head and shoulders of a young man who was blended into the altered state of trance. I watched as the energy became denser around the gentleman and then, all of a sudden, I started to see lots of little movements within the mass of energy.

The energy started to become a little more transparent and then I was aware of three fully formed miniature spirit people roughly about twelve inches in height on the back of the armchair! One of the figures was standing on the left shoulder of the gentleman, another was walking across the back frame of the armchair and the other was sitting on the gentleman's right shoulder!

I was intrigued with what I was seeing. I just gazed in amazement at what was happening in front of me. I watched these wonderful phenomena taking place around the gentleman for about five minutes, and then the energy changed and they were no longer visible to me.

When we are dealing with the spirit world, it is important to keep an open mind. This experience was wonderful and showed me that they have the ability to manipulate the energy to show themselves in any size or form that they choose.

I was working with a lady at another trance workshop and was very much aware of a gentleman who was working with her from the spirit side of life. I watched as the gentleman showed himself standing behind her and then brought his energy forward to blend into hers. I was aware as I connected into the energy of what was taking place between them that the gentleman was a druid.

I was able to communicate with the gentleman without the medium being aware of what was taking place and the information that came from him was incredible. He was a man of the earth, connected into nature and was able to show me a little bit of his life when he was on the material world.

The following day, I decided to run a physical development class with the group and asked the same lady to go into the séance cabinet under red light conditions through the direction of my own guides. The lady went into the cabinet and I watched as the same gentleman who was with her the previous day appeared behind her and started to blend into her energy.

A short time had passed within the blending process when, to my great surprise, a mass of energy started to appear around the head and shoulders of the medium in the cabinet. The energy appeared to be grey in colour and moved across the inside of the cabinet. It looked like a moving mist and then it completely formed over the head of the medium. I watched intently as the energy of the mist became thicker in volume and then the medium's face disappeared within it.

Suddenly, the medium's face reappeared visible to everyone within the séance room. Her face started to morph in and out of the energy within the mist, as if it was starting to rearrange its appearance. I watched in amazement at what was happening and, within a few minutes of watching the medium's face coming and going within the mist of energy, the energy became a solid mass around the medium's head and I was now looking at a cat's face instead of the medium's face in the cabinet.

The image of the cat's head where the medium's head should have been stayed visible to the whole group for about five minutes within the confinements of the séance cabinet, before the energy started to dissipate and the medium was asked to release the guide from her energy and for the guide to return back to his side of life.

This turn of events was a wonderful experience not just for me to witness but also for the whole group who took part that day. I have got to know this particular guide of the medium very well over the last few years. The information received from him has been noted, searched and verified when applicable by the medium, who has a particular interest in paganism, druids and witches.

Apparently druids have the ability to transform into animal guides.

I have witnessed facial hair and full heads of hair appear around individuals as the energy forms around them when they have been sitting in séance cabinets for development. This type of phenomena has been witnessed by the whole group who were observing the proceedings.

Phenomena can happen with anyone when sitting in a séance cabinet and also have been known to take place, when the energy is correct, while sitting for trance in daylight. I always find that when this happens it is a remarkable achievement for all involved in both sides of life.

I have had the pleasure of watching people sitting in the altered state who have appeared to stretch and shrink within the energy. I have witnessed and felt spirit children, elemental beings, nature spirits, bright lights, columns of energy that have appeared and moved about the room independently. I have seen spirit faces that have appeared and moved indiscriminately within the energy contained in the room that were approximately the size of a fifty pence piece.

I'm delighted that I have been given the opportunity to work with people within all levels of their development in the altered states, and I think that to be able to help them with their journey is a privilege and an honour.

I could continue writing all day about the experiences that I have witnessed with spirit energy and the students who work hard to develop with the altered state of trance. But, for now, maybe I will keep that for another book.

The most crucial part of your development within trance mediumship is that you enjoy what takes place with the blending energy of your guides. If you do not enjoy it, then don't do it. One of the most important things to remember is that you cannot hurry any stages of your development. The energy that they bring to you through the blending process is controlled by your guides and they will develop you.

I have tried lots of different ways to try to quicken my development over the years and I eventually succumbed to the understanding that it is best to leave that side of things to my spirit team.

When you are developing, it is more than likely that you will see little progression made with your hard work at the beginning. I found that keeping a journal helped me to see how far I had travelled on my path.

The art to developing trance mediumship is not to give up but to persevere no matter how much you get frustrated with yourself or the spirit world.

Séance Cabinet Work

Cabinet work is associated with the development of physical mediumship. Physical mediumship is a passion of mine that I have been actively involved in for many years. It is the ultimate proof of the existence of the spirit world when developed and demonstrated correctly.

The purpose of the séance cabinet is to condense the spirit energy within the confinements of the structure of the cabinet. The construction of the cabinet is usually three sided with a drape that can be used to cover the front, if required. When looking at many of the physical séances that were conducted in the past, however, the construction of the cabinet was just a couple of curtains hung up over the side of a corner in a darkened room.

Physical mediumship is very rare within the spiritual community. It was rare a hundred years ago and it is no different today. This type of mediumship takes years and years of hard work and dedication to develop properly and you must have that special quality which lies within your chemical make-up that makes you a physical medium.

It saddens me to say that if you don't have that special quality of physical mediumship energy within your chemical make-up, then you will never be able to fully develop physical mediumship.

Common Questions

There are some concerns and issues that seem to come up regularly when people are having discussions on physical mediumship. One that can arise with this particular type of mediumship is why this usually has to be demonstrated or developed within pitch dark conditions or under the direction of a red light shining into the cabinet, although blue and green lights can be used.

I believe that the reason for this is to do with the manipulation of the energy needed to demonstrate this type of mediumship. This particular type of rare mediumship is normally conducted in darkened conditions or under certain coloured light conditions so that the guides and helpers from the spirit side of life can bring their energy forward for us to blend with. In doing so, they create a vibrational physical energy from their side into our world through the blending energy and vibration made through the contact with the physical medium.

The darkened conditions make it easier for them to manipulate the vibration around us when in the séance cabinet and, when coloured light is introduced, they have to manipulate the vibration again to accommodate the change created within the energy and light with the use of the coloured bulbs.

When white light or direct daylight is introduced into the proceedings taking place within the darkened room, this change in the light source has the ability to interfere with the vibration of the energy contained within the cabinet, and can inhibit any phenomena that is being developed or being presented through the energy with or around the medium in the room.

Another topic that is often discussed is the pioneers of the past who demonstrated this very rare type of mediumship and how they underwent rigorous tests to prove that their mediumship was honest and genuine.

Unfortunately, these mediums of the past who demonstrated this wonderful gift of physical mediumship are sadly no longer around in the material world. Furthermore, the majority of people who were privileged to witness these wonderful phenomena are also no longer around today to share their experiences with us. This is causing problems within the demonstration of physical mediumship today as the people attending the demonstrations for physical are not sure what they are actually witnessing because they have nothing to compare it to.

There are still a few people around today who have been privileged to experience genuine physical mediumship demonstrations with the late Gordon Higginson. I have had the pleasure to sit with a few of these people and listen to the stories of wonderful evidence that they witnessed with him through ectoplasmic materialisation of loved ones and communication through independent voice. These phenomena left them with no doubt within their minds that the proceedings they had witnessed was the ultimate proof of life being eternal.

The physical mediums of today are not tried and tested like the mediums of the past and the physical evidence is not the same. This is why it is so important for people looking to demonstrate physical mediumship to dedicate time to their development and not take it out to the public before it is fully matured and ready.

I do believe that there are small groups of people today who are quietly developing physical mediumship. These people have reverted back to the old ways of sitting behind closed doors in small, dedicated circles. These groups are taking the time and allowing themselves to develop at the right pace through the guidance of the spirit world.

Light Force Energy

The spirit world is developing a new way of showing physical mediumship that they are calling "light force energy". This new type of energy is less harmful to the medium and will be developed through time.

This energy has a light source that is seemingly being developed within the energy and vibration that is connected to the medium. The light source will be attached to the medium so séances in the dark will be a thing of the past.

The group who I sit with have observed columns of grey light that have appeared in the darkened room where we sit for development, and we have witnessed four columns moving about in a criss-cross pattern. The group has also witnessed one column of light appear and stretch from the floor to the ceiling, which is approximately twelve feet in height, then shrink to half the size and return back to its full length. We have also witnessed strips of light appear within the energy created in the séance room and have watched them condense into thin rods.

The information we have received from the spirit world is that the columns will be developed with the medium's energy and vibration, and can be used to form a portal to gaze into their world. This column of light will enable you and your loved ones to view each other and you will be able to communicate with them.

This new way of developing energy is exciting to be part of but I am under no illusion that it will be quite some time before it is ready to be demonstrated to the public, and to be honest it may never be in my lifetime.

I am not saying that ectoplasm will be a thing of the past in physical séances. We may experience the spirit world continuing to use it with certain mediums, and we may see both types being used at the same time with other mediums. I suppose the thing we must remember is that the spirit world does not sit idle, they are always looking at ways to advance technology to enhance our development.

This new type of energy being developed is not just confined to physical mediumship, it is also being introduced into the healing side and is being called "**life** force healing energy" to differentiate between its use within healing and physical mediumship.

I will elaborate more about this type of healing energy later in another chapter.

Elementals In Physical Séances

I remember sitting one evening in the séance cabinet for development, when I felt the energy around me begin to change. This time the energy felt different and I began to have the feeling come upon me of beginning to shrink in the seat.

I began to feel that my body and limbs were starting to become twisted in all different directions, and it was as if my arms and fingers were becoming something else. I could hear members of the group saying, "Look at that! The medium is becoming smaller."

There was a deep silence in the room for quite some time, then someone said, "Look at that, that's a tree spirit!"

I remember having the feeling that I was small in size and felt that my body and limbs had become twisted and gnarly like the branches of an old tree. This little elemental visitor who was blending with me did not speak, he just wanted to show himself to the group. When his energy dissipated from my energy and I returned out of the altered state, it was apparent to me that it certainly caused a bit of a stir amongst the group that evening.

The group have become aware of elementals who are now regular visitors to the séance room. It is always announced by our guides that they are coming forward and not to try to touch them.

The group members are aware of them and can feel their energy and see their shapes through the energy contained within the room. Some of them look like little tree creatures with twigs for fingers and others look a little different in appearance.

The spirit guides always mention that, when these elementals appear into our world, their energy and vibration is slightly different to that of the spirit world. The energy they bring with them has a feeling that it is hot and electrically charged within the vibration of the room.

I was in Ireland one weekend running a mentorship class and I was asked to go into the cabinet by the group. I had been in the cabinet for a short time when my guide spoke and told the group that they were going to bring forward elementals.

The guide explained that under no circumstances was anyone to try to touch any of them, and asked that the group just enjoy the experience of the feeling of the different energy as it would be like nothing they had witnessed before.

Afterwards, the group discussed what they had seen and experienced within the energy, and what the guide had said to them. They all agreed that they had felt an energy and witnessed things that they had never experienced before.

The guide had said to the group that the energy associated with the elementals would feel like pins and needles coming over the physical body. I still laugh today when I think about the two men who were sitting in the group that evening after they both cautiously explained that they had both felt pins and needles all over their bodies and had experienced a burning sensation, but only in their backsides!

The most important thing to remember with cabinet work is that the energy and vibration must be controlled at all times by your spirit team. Each time you sit for trance it is an experiment and we can never be sure what will take place.

We have found that when elementals have been brought forward into the séance room, they have always been introduced to the group by a member of my spirit team. They always alert us to the understanding that they are being brought forward, and to maintain certain guidelines that must be strictly adhered to.

Elemental beings are the most intriguing little creatures and must be respected at all times as they come from their own plane of existence or their own vibrational world and no-one really knows a lot about them. The one thing that we have learned about them is that they do not come from or live in the spirit world. Their place of existence is a different dimension. I shall touch upon where they may exist later in another chapter.

Struggling To Return Back To Your Body
In The Cabinet

I was sitting one evening with my weekly development group

and it was my turn to go into the cabinet. I got into the cabinet, sat down in the chair and very quickly I felt the blending with my guide taking control.

Within a few minutes, I was deep into an altered state and found myself having a private conversation with one of my guides. We were walking along a beautiful sandy beach which was a million miles away from where I was sitting in the séance room in Edinburgh.

I had become aware that someone from the spirit side of life was speaking to the group members through me, whilst I was sitting in the cabinet, but what the conversation was about, I can't recall.

I remember hearing the voice of the guide saying, "We are going to return the medium back to you." I then felt my energy slowly being pulled back in the direction of the chair where I was sitting. When I arrived back in the cabinet, I found myself standing alongside my physical body and I was looking at myself in the cabinet.

I was standing outside of my physical body and I could not connect back into it. At this point, I started to panic. I could feel my heart starting to race. I was having palpitations. I was starting to get worried. The fear factor of being stuck outside my body forever was making my mind spiral out of control.

Then I heard the familiar voice of Henry. He said, "Do not panic, everything is under control. You will return back into your body in due course. Just stay calm and breathe."

I could hear the guide speaking once again through me from the cabinet as I was standing to the side of my physical body. He was explaining to the group members that they were having a little difficulty returning the medium and asked for them to be patient as they reshuffled the energy to re-establish the connection.

I was just standing there waiting for what seemed like an eternity! All I could do was to continue to breathe in a controlled manner under the direction of Henry's guidance and wait patiently trying not to get in a panic.

I heard the guide saying, "Everything is OK. We are now going to return the medium to you." I started to feel myself slowly returning back into my physical body within the cabinet. It felt like my energy was gently floating back in stages and, every second this was taking place, I was becoming more aware that my consciousness was returning to being me once again.

I sat in the cabinet after this experience for quite some time before I spoke to the group about my ordeal. I was just relieved that I was back safely after this scary incident. This had never happened to me before and I was quite frightened.

The trust I have in Henry is what got me through this challenge. His guidance has always been instrumental in my development, and I trust him like a father figure. This has happened a few times over the course of my development, and now when it happens, I don't panic, I just wait until I feel the energy slowly return back to my physical body under the control of my spirit team.

I have, over the years, experienced many wonderful places that my guides have taken me to when I have been sitting for development. I have found myself walking along many beautiful beaches while talking with my guides and have gazed across the most spectacular views from the top of mountains. I have also had the sensation of soaring on the backs of eagles looking at the world we live in from high above.

I have visited many libraries or halls of learning. On a few occasions, I have even found myself sitting in front of lots of television screens and watching myself in different time zones from different periods in my life that have unfolded in front of my own eyes like a storybook.

What Is A Title?

I've never had any interest in getting caught up with titles that people give you or hung up on a name of a pioneering guide that everyone knows and talks about from the past. I have always believed that any guide or spirit worker who comes to work with you is special in their own way. Their vibrational energy will be compatible with your own energy and they will be trained on the spirit side of life to do the work through you to the best of their ability.

The title of "psychic surgeon" was given to me by members of the spiritual community who had become aware of the people from the spirit side of life who were coming forward to work through me within the healing side of my mediumistic journey.

I never gave myself this title and, to be honest, I only think of myself as a HEALER. I do, however, find it amusing when I read about people telling the public that they have now decided to be known as a "psychic surgeon". Psychic surgery is gift given to you from the spirit world; it is not a title that you take for yourself because you decide you want to be known as that type of healer.

People should be content with the path that they have chosen on their spiritual journey and not get hung up with titles. We should put more focus into being the best channel we can be for those on the spirit side of life to work through us. Ultimately, all we are is a channel or vessel for the energy to pass through. We are only the bridge that connects the energy between the two worlds.

Always remember there are no titles in the spirit world, titles are man-made.

The Start Of My Journey With Healing

In this section of the book, I will share my understanding of my spiritual path through the guidance of my spirit guides and communicators into the world of healing and the wonderful experiences and results that can take place when you trust them.

I would like to start with my first encounter in the strange world of psychic surgery that would change my life as I knew it. A lady got in touch for a healing through a mutual acquaintance. The lady explained over the telephone that she was a working medium and had been suffering with a few health conditions over a long period of time. An appointment was arranged for the lady come to my home.

I had spent four and a half years developing trance and trance healing with my guides behind closed doors; I had not held any healing clinics for strangers before. The only healings that I had done were with family and friends behind closed doors.

I was nervous when the lady arrived for her appointment and, after the pleasantries were exchanged, I asked her if she was ready to begin. The lady got on top of the healing bed that I had organised in my living room. I did not have any healing clinics at the time. I sat in the power for a short period of time allowing the energy around me to settle. I then invited my healing guides to come forward. I felt the energy of the blending with the vibration of one of my healing guides taking place with my own vibration, and the healing commenced.

After a short period of time had passed, I felt the energy of the healing guide change around me and I realised that I was now standing outside my own physical body watching the proceedings. I watched in disbelief as, all of a sudden, a lady nurse appeared out of the vibration and wheeled in a tray of surgical instruments on a trolley. Then the healing guide who was working through me raised up my physical body so it was standing up out of the chair and leaned over to position it over the lady's head. The guide lifted spiritual surgical instruments up out of the tray and proceeded to remove the lady's (spirit) eye and place it on a small silver tray. The spirit surgeon then carefully performed some delicate work on the back of the spirit eye as it lay on the tray.

Once the necessary work had been performed, the spirit surgeon replaced the spirit eye back into the lady's spirit eye socket. At this point, the energy changed once again and another blending took place. A second surgeon came forward and, working through me, picked up an instrument from the tray and made an incision into what he led me to believe was the thyroid gland (in the spiritual body of the lady). Within a few minutes the surgery was complete and he left as quickly as he had arrived. I felt the energy of the blending of the guide start to retract, and at this point I started to feel my vibration return back into my own body. I gently brought myself out of the altered state and asked the lady to bring her conscious mind back into the room.

The lady said that she had become aware of lots of spirit people around her as she lay upon the healing bed, and she had felt that her eye had been worked upon. She also explained that she had the feeling as if someone had tried to make an incision into her throat area.

Although the lady had discussed in detail what she had felt and experienced within the healing session, I found it peculiar that she had made reference to having the feeling of being in a hospital environment and the sensation of receiving an operation taking place on her physical body.

Later that evening, I took time to reflect upon the proceedings of the healing session with the lady. I could not quite understand what had taken place in the healing session at my home.

Who were these new guides who are working with me? I kept thinking over and over to myself. What if the events I had witnessed during the healing were just a figment of my imagination? Had I managed to interfere with the proceedings that had taken place through my own thoughts and desires to help the lady? Had I somehow taken over the control of the blending process? Was this real? Why had my spirit come out of my physical body? Was it so that I could watch and understand what was taking place with the healers working through me? This all was a new experience in my journey. I did not understand any of it, and I questioned it constantly in my mind.

I decided to look for information on psychic surgery. The books I managed to find in the beginning of my quest for knowledge were all about psychic surgeons from the Philippines who appeared to carry out operations which removed certain items of organic matter from the physical bodies of clients.

This was nothing like I had experienced. There was no blood or gore involved with what had taken place with me. All work had been carried out on the spiritual body of the lady. I did eventually manage to find a couple of books after extensive research. Although the books were interesting to read, they did not really help me find the answers I was seeking.

Psychic Surgeons Are Physical Mediums

Through my extensive investigations and enquiries with many healers and experienced mediums involved in the field of trance, it came to light that the gift of psychic surgery is a very rare phenomenon. To be a psychic surgeon you must have the correct chemical composition contained within your DNA that enables the spirit world to take the entranced medium into another deeper dimension of blending which is necessary for physical mediumship.

Physical mediums and the energy they carry with them are rare. Psychic surgery is an advancement of trance healing mediumship. This type of healing phenomenon has always been and, always will be, very unusual amongst trance healing mediums. It can take years and years of dedication for this type of mediumship to be developed to a standard to be able to represent it out in public on behalf of the spirit world. It cannot be developed quickly, and your healing spirit team must have complete control over the medium in the altered state of trance.

Psychic surgery is a gift that can only be bestowed upon you by the spirit world. This type of phenomenon must be developed in a controlled safe environment.

Be Honest

I explain to every client who comes to see me, or makes an enquiry for a healing session, that I cannot guarantee to cure any disease or ailment that they may be suffering with. I always make it clear to them that I am only the vessel or channel for my spirit team to work through. I only open myself to a divine energy source which allows those from the spirit side of life the opportunity to come forward to see what they can do to help.

The Healing Journey Continues

I decided to just accept what had taken place with the healing surgery with the lady that day and looked forward with intrigue to what lay ahead.

Confirmation

I remember getting in touch with the gentleman who was my tutor and trying to explain to him what I had experienced while working with the lady. You must remember that this was a new experience for me. We spoke in great detail about what had taken place and then we came to the conclusion that he would receive a healing from me next time we arranged to come together at a workshop.

The day came for us to meet up at the prearranged workshop. I had not done any other healings since the healing with the lady. I had, however, sat regular as clockwork with the spirit world, five times a week within the blending process.

The workshop progressed along steadily in the morning with all the group in attendance blending with their guides in the altered states of trance. In the afternoon, the tutor asked me to give him a healing. He lay on a healing bed and I sat at the end of the bed like I usually do.

I felt the energy come forward and the blending with the guide begin. I remember rising from the chair and moving down the bed with my hands raised above the body of the tutor. I hovered my hands above the stomach area for a short time and then, once again, the energy changed and I was standing alongside my physical body. I became aware of the nurse, wearing an old-style uniform, wheeling in a tray of surgical instruments.

The gentleman, or should I say surgeon, who was working through me proceeded to lift spiritual instruments from the tray and began to make an incision into the spiritual body of the tutor. I watched what was taking place during the operation although my physical eyes were closed at all times.

I did not know how long the operation had taken. I just remember the energy drawing me back into my physical body and, after a few minutes, I was asking the tutor to gently bring his consciousness back into the room. I waited for a few minutes for the tutor to bring himself fully back. I was intrigued to hear his insight into what had taken place.

The first thing he said was that he could feel things getting moved within his physical body. He could feel the energy going straight through his body and that someone was working on his spinal area. He could also smell hospital conditions including iodine. Then other people of the group said that they could also smell iodine within the room.

The tutor then said, "I have no doubt in saying that what I have just experienced is psychic surgery." That statement of confirmation from him meant a lot to me. I returned back to my seat with the understanding in my mind that this new stage in my healing journey was not a figment of my imagination. This was real.

A New Chapter Opens Up In My Development

I was at a seminar in Wales for an experimental trance retreat.

I was there with a few friends who I already knew and some others who I had never met until this event. Everyone who was present on the retreat were either working mediums in their own right or had been actively involved in trance mediumship development for quite a few years.

The tutor on the course asked me to carry out a healing. The healing was to take place in front of the whole group later in the afternoon. The tutor said, "I want to see how your development has continued from what took place at the last workshop." I was reluctant to carry out the healing in front of strangers but I knew I had no way of getting myself out of it!

The afternoon came and I was asked to work with a few of the group members. The first person chosen from the group was a lady who had been suffering with a pain in the head. I asked the lady to lie on the healing bed. I then asked her to take in three deep breaths to enable me to make the connection with her spirit.

I felt the blending of the energy take hold immediately, and I began to go deeper and deeper into the altered state of trance. I became aware of spirit people standing around the bed; they were observing and discussing the patient. I felt an energy change within the blending and I became aware of a tray of instruments that were being pushed in alongside the bed by a nurse with an older style uniform on.

The spirit surgeon who was working through me proceeded to work on the spiritual head of the lady. My eyes were closed but I could see what was taking place. This time I was aware that I was now standing to the left-hand side of my physical body. I was outside my physical body looking at myself and observing the proceedings as they unfolded. I watched as the surgeon made an incision into the skin around the lady's spiritual head and pulled back what appeared to be her scalp downwards to the bottom of the back of her skull.

He then picked up an instrument that looked like a hand

drill with a circular saw blade at the end. He then placed or lined up the saw blade onto the spiritual skull of the lady and proceeded to slowly cut into the bone. He turned the handle at the side of the instrument very delicately and it started to cut in a circular motion.

After a few minutes, he put the drill down and then removed a small circular disc of bone that he had cut out from the lady's spiritual skull and laid it onto a silver-looking dish to his right. He then proceeded to pick up very thin-looking spiritual instruments, and started to very carefully push them into the brain mass, through the hole he had cut away in the skull. I was mesmerised with what was taking place.

This gentleman was using my physical body to carry out a spiritual operation through the blending with spirit. After a short time had passed, the gentleman put the instruments down, and he lifted the piece of skull that he had removed previously up from the dish and delicately placed it back into where it had come from in the lady's skull.

He then secured it back in place, and used a solution that he put around the circular line where the bone had been removed and replaced. He then lifted the hair back from the rear of the lady's head, and lined up the scalp and then sealed it with what looked like stitches.

I then felt the energy change and I was no longer standing to the side of my physical body. I was now back in my body with my hands raised above the head of the lady. After a few minutes, I felt the energy start to draw back from me and I was back in the room with the group.

The lady stated that she could feel the energy around her. She was aware of her surroundings at all times, but was unable to move when she was on the bed. She also said that she could feel a sharp pain at one point in her head.

The second group member was a man who had a problem in his lower region. I asked the gentleman to lie on the healing bed that had been put up in the room directly in front of the other members of the group so they could observe what was taking place, and I then proceeded to make him comfortable.

I asked him to breathe in deeply three times and made the connection with his spirit. I remember closing my eyes and having the feeling of the trance energy coming around me as the guide started taking control into my energy.

After a short spell, I felt myself starting to rise out of the chair and move down the side of the bed with my eyes closed. I was once again aware of spirit people around the bed. There were two nurses this time. They were dressed in older type uniforms, standing at the other side of the bed along with what appeared to be people who looked like surgeons. Amongst these spirit people there were trays of surgical instruments neatly arranged on silver-looking trays.

I could see the spirit surgeon who was working through me reach for a cloth that seemed to be sodden in a solution and wipe it over the spiritual body that had risen about 18 inches above the physical body of the gentleman lying on the bed. Then the surgeon reached for a spiritual instrument and made an incision into the area of the group member's spiritual body that was causing him discomfort. Silver-looking clamps were inserted into the area of the incision.

The guide who was working through me proceeded to work meticulously with great attention to detail. I watched him intently as he used different instruments that he picked up from the silver tray with no sense of urgency. I was intrigued as he appeared to work inside the spiritual body of the patient, and was removing and attaching certain pieces of anatomy.

I became aware of the clamps being removed and what appeared to be stitches being put along the area of where the operation had taken place. When the stitching was complete, the area was once again wiped with the cloth with the iodine solution. I observed that the spiritual body was gently lowered back into the physical body and I felt the energy start to withdraw back from me.

To my horror, when my consciousness had returned back into the room, I found myself facing the opposite direction of the gentleman who was lying on the bed. I had turned round 180 degrees on the people watching the proceedings, so now I had my back to them. I thought to myself as I looked at the wall, "What have I done? I've interfered in the proceedings and now I've made a fool of myself in front of about 14 people." I stood there cringing. I did not want to turn round but I knew I had to.

When I eventually turned around, everyone started to laugh. I could see the gentleman lying on the bed with his eyes closed. I could feel my face becoming redder and redder with embarrassment. I wanted a big hole to appear and swallow me up! Talk about embarrassment!

The tutor said, "Anything wrong?" I just looked around at everyone laughing. I was mortified. "Ask the patient what he felt," was the next statement from the tutor. I asked the gentleman how he was feeling and what he had experienced during the healing.

To my amazement, he described how he could feel the energy of the spirit world immediately as I asked him to breathe in three times. He went on to explain that he had become aware of the feeling of being in hospital conditions. He also stated to the group that he was strangely aware of what felt like an incision being made into his physical body and things being moved around internally. He went on to say that this for him was a bizarre experience as he felt he had received an operation. I remember looking back at the wall and wondering how could he possibly feel this when I was facing the wrong way?

The tutor asked, "Do you know what has just happened?" "No," was my reply. "The spirit world was experimenting with you. They had raised the spiritual body of the patient who you were working with and had moved it away from his physical body. That is how you ended up facing the wall with your back to us. You have done nothing wrong. You were completely under their control and deep enough that you did not interfere at all with the connection."

My initial reaction was one of shock and embarrassment. However, in hindsight, it was comforting to know that I had done nothing wrong. What had taken place was another part of learning on my journey. They had done this so I could start to understand more about the workings of the spirit world and what they are more than capable of doing with us when we give ourselves over to them.

What I did not know at the time of the healing was that, amongst the group members on the course, there were two people who were trained operating theatre nurses. These people both mentioned that what they had witnessed while watching the first healing that had taken place was similar to what they experience on a day-to-day basis in their field of work.

They had been able to perceive through their clairvoyance and openly commented that they had watched the spirit workers build up a framework around the lady's head to secure it for non-movement before the operation began. The other members of the group also mentioned that they could smell iodine in the air.

I was asked to work with a lady who had recently been diagnosed and treated for meningitis. Although she had recovered from the condition, it had left her with other ailments. I worked with this lady in private in a separate room over a few days on the course. She had been having problems with memory and getting her words mixed up and back to front on emails and texts.

On the first healing that took place, I became aware of a spirit doctor blending with me and lifting my hands onto the head of the lady who was lying on the bed. I soon became aware of energy that felt alive transmitting through my hands and into the head of the lady. Then I became aware that they were showing me a picture of the inside of the lady's head. I was being shown what looked like currents of electricity that were running through and across her brain.

They then drew my attention to a part of the brain where the surge of electricity appeared to arch as if it was jumping and not flowing naturally. I watched in my mind's eye as the surgeons controlled the current of energy from arching inside the lady's head.

This was a wonderful opportunity for me to experiment with the spirit doctors and surgeons. This lady was a working medium and it gave me the opportunity not only to work with my spirit team, but also it gave them the freedom to have conversations with the lady through trance communication to explain to her what was going on with her condition.

The following day the lady advised me that she had slept very well through the night after receiving the healing. She also divulged that she was having heart palpitations, and asked if I thought my spirit team could possibly have a look at this. I explained to her that I did not have control of what they would or could do. All I could do was put the thought out to them and see what unfolded.

Once again, the lady got on to the healing bed and, before I could ask her to take an intake of breath, I was aware that there were two spirit doctors standing behind me discussing her as she lay on the bed. I told her that I was listening to two gentlemen standing behind me discussing her and the plan of action they were going to take. She said that she was aware of them and could hear them speaking.

I asked her to draw an intake of breath and I started to feel the connection through the energy to her spirit. I went into an altered state and, like clockwork, I saw the nurse arrive with the trolley with the spiritual instruments on top. I then noticed a surgeon standing at the other side of the bed. This gentleman was different in appearance to anyone who had arrived to work with me up to now. He appeared to have a metal-looking disc that was brass in colour attached to the front of his forehead. This brass disc had something attached at the front of it like a candle that seemed to shine a light.

I felt myself lifting from the chair and moving down the side of the bed. There were quite a few spirit people around the vicinity of the bed. The surgeon, who was working through me, took a cloth dipped in a solution from the tray of instruments and proceeded to wipe it over the spirit chest area of the lady whose spirit body, at this stage, had risen up about a foot above her physical body.

He took a scalpel and made an incision into her spiritual chest and then used something that looked like a clamp to open up her chest so her heart was exposed. He picked up an instrument and appeared to clamp it onto one side of the heart and then another onto the other side, and then he proceeded to work with her heart for a few minutes.

Another instrument was picked up from the tray and also used on the heart. I believe this was something to restart the heartbeat. At this point, there was another gentleman who appeared and checked that the heart was beating normally. The surgeon then started to remove all the instruments that had been used around the heart and put them back on to a tray. Then he used an instrument that appeared to wash the whole area where he had been working with a solution.

The surgeon removed the clamp-looking instrument and proceeded to put everything back together, finishing with inserting stitches into the chest and sewing the area up. When this task had been completed, once again the area of the body they had worked on was washed with the cloth with the solution on it. I felt the energy start to draw back from me and gently, after a few minutes, I was back.

I leant forward and gently touched the lady on the face to bring her back. We spoke in great detail about what had just happened.

To my amazement, the lady said that she was aware that an operation had taken place on her heart. She explained that she had been shown through her mediumistic ability the procedure that had been carried out when she was lying on the healing bed.

The last healing I did with the lady was directed by the influence of my spirit team. I was asked by them to involve another few members of the group on the course. I picked a couple of people who I knew were trance healers, and asked if they would participate with me in a joint healing with the lady who I had been working with over the last few days.

The next day we all met up in the room I had been using for the healing. I asked one of them to stand at the bottom of the bed and the other to stand at the middle of the bed, and I would take the position at the end where the lady's head would be. I explained that we were going to experiment, with the help of the spirit world, with the healing which was going to take place with the lady.

My spirit team had asked that we all go into an altered state of trance and allow our healers to come forward and work together to assist. A few minutes after we had discussed what we were trying to achieve with the guidance of the spirit world, the lady arrived and I asked her to lie on the bed and then we took up our positions around the bed.

I asked her to take in three deep breaths, and then I asked her to allow her breathing to return to a normal pace that was comfortable for her. I then indicated to the two members of the group to begin. I felt the trance energy come forward as my guide blended with me. I was aware of lots of colours that were appearing in my mind and I knew that they were for the lady receiving the joint healing.

I don't know how long the healing went on for but, after a period of time, I felt the energy draw back from me. I opened my eyes and, to my surprise, the other two healers and the lady were starting to come back from their blending with the energy.

The strangest thing was that we had all come back within 20 or 30 seconds of each other. The lady explained she felt that she had been bombarded with energy from all sides and had experienced lots of healing colours.

The experiment was to show the intelligence behind the healing energy and our spirit guides. How they were able to control the healing and bring each of us back from the altered state at the same time all under their control.

This trance seminar had given me lots to think about. Not only had it given me the opportunity to experiment with trance and psychic surgery in a safe environment with experienced trance mediums, it had given me confidence to trust what I was doing was right, and also it brought a new and profound understanding. I had lots and lots of development still to do. I had only dipped my toe into the pool of knowledge but through the understanding and guidance which consistently came from my spirit team, I looked forward to the challenges that lay ahead.

When I returned home from the seminar, I was in a high spirits! It had been an amazing experience for me. Not just with the healing that I had partaken in but also getting to know more people who had the same interest and love for the altered states of trance.

I went back to sitting at home with those from spirit once again. I dedicated five days a week for an average time of one and a half hours a day, surrendering my thoughts to them without interfering which, I must say, can be a challenge. It takes discipline not just from us as we go forward to develop, but there must also be discipline from those who come forward to work with us.

Experimenting With Trance Healing

I met up with one of my friends a few weeks later and we decided to allow spirit to experiment with us. I got my friend to lie on the healing bed and I went into an altered state of trance. Within a few minutes of the blending taking place with me, spirit activity within the room had become very busy. I had become aware of a number of spirit people standing around the bed.

I felt that this time the blending with spirit was quite light and I proceeded to stand up at the side of the bed with my friend lying horizontally in front of me. The energy that started to come through my hands felt like electricity discharging through my fingertips. The energy was alive and had a strange substance to it which felt dense. I started to wriggle my fingers, and it had the feeling like shards of electricity were dripping like droplets of rain coming through the ends of my fingers.

I started to become aware of colour that was coming through my hands: greens, blues, oranges and yellows that were hovering and flowing about like mist above the physical body of my friend. When I moved my hands in any direction, the colours seemed to move with me. I had become one with the energy flow emitting all around my friend.

I was playing with the energy or spirit were playing with my hands in the energy to be more exact. The energy was reacting to the direction of movement made by my hands, like an orchestra reacts to the commands of the conductor. I was fascinated with what they were doing and showing me. I was caught up within this movement of the energy for quite some time.

I then felt a shift in the energy, and my hands lowered downwards towards the physical body of my friend. I felt the energy change once more as my hands moved towards the area of my friend's lower tummy. The energy started to feel heavier and, all of a sudden, the energy locked onto the bladder area. My hands would not budge from this area. It appeared that the energy coming through my hands at this time had another purpose.

Suddenly, my hands lifted upwards and, in my mind's eye, I was becoming aware of the spirit bladder of my friend rising out of her physical body. It rose about a foot above her physical body, which was lying on the healing bed. To be honest, I was in awe of the experience. I then thought to myself, "Am I imagining this in my mind?" Then, all of a sudden, my physical hand, under the direction of the person working through me, lightly squeezed the spirit bladder which, in due course, woke my friend up from her slumber and she said, "I'm really sorry but I really need to go to the bathroom."

What a strange turn of events this afternoon had turned out to be. Not just the experience of being part of the flow of the healing energy, but questioning myself about seeing and feeling the spirit bladder rise from my friend's physical body, and then having my spirit team providing the evidence to me by squeezing the bladder to confirm that what I was experiencing and seeing was real.

I never did any more experiments with healing with my friend but we still remain on good terms today. We often talk about what took place on that day and the experience of someone or something grabbing on to her bladder, that made her need to relieve herself.

I've always held the belief that, when working with spirit, I have the understanding that every time they come forward to work with us, it will be an experiment. It would be small-minded of us to believe that every time they come forward to work with us the experience will be the same, as we never know who is going to be the guide or spirit worker nominated for the task. The only thing we can be sure of when working with spirit, is that the right people will come when they are needed.

I've always experimented with the spirit world through my healing journey after that experience with my friend. I think it is important as a healer to understand as much as possible about how healing energy works.

Although I have a better understanding today than when I first started my healing journey, I still think of myself as a novice when we talk about the knowledge and skill that those from the spirit side of life have regarding the working of the healing energy.

I always take the opportunity to experiment with healing energy but only through the direction of my guides. I was working with a friend and the feeling of the energy that was transmitting through my hands felt like pins and needles. I asked my wife, Gail, to come forward and feel the energy.

Gail put her hand under my hand and she could feel the sensation of pins and needles through the energy created through the blending process. I then asked her to lower her hand and I put my left hand in between her hand and under my right hand. Gail could still feel the energy of pins and needles tapping onto her hand, and then I asked my friend, who was lying on the healing bed, if she could feel the energy. She also could feel the sensation of pins and needles.

When a healing is taking place, it is not normal for the energy to be felt through the contact of someone else intervening within the flow of energy. The client receiving the healing will feel the energy but it is not the case for the person putting their hand in between the flow. The healing energy is for the client and not for the person intervening with the flow. When asking the spirit world to experiment, they have always shown me different ways that the energy works.

Another experiment that I would like to share is how the healing energy has the ability to transmit from one area to another within the body. I was experimenting with another friend who has a great interest in healing. I put my hand onto her left knee and asked the spirit world to heat up her right knee. Within a few minutes, my friend started to feel her right knee beginning to heat up although there was no contact apart from my hand upon her left knee.

This little experiment gave me a better understanding of how to work with a situation that arose with a client a few months later. The client had got in touch with me because she had tremendous pain in her leg.

When I arrived at the client's home, she was bed bound. I spoke to the client and asked her (under the direction of my guide) if it was OK to put my hands onto her left knee. The problem was that it was her right leg that was causing her concern and she was lying on a bed that was against the wall which meant I could not reach over to her right leg.

After I was given permission, I put my hands onto her left knee and, almost immediately, she felt the spirit world working upon her right knee. I worked on her left knee for about ten minutes and, when the healing session was complete, the client said that she felt great relief from the pain.

There is a particular experiment I do with my groups so that they feel and understand the intelligence behind the healing energy. I get my groups to sit as a threesome, one behind the other. I ask two of the group members to sit in the same direction and the other group member to be facing them.

I then ask those in the groups to close their eyes, and ask that the person at the back of the row go into the blending process with their healing guide and begin to send the healing energy directly to the person who is facing towards the other group members in the row.

I then ask the person sitting in the middle of the row to become aware of where the healing energy travels round about them. I ask them to become aware of the sensation of the energy coming around them, over them or through them.

This exercise has never failed to produce results. The person in the middle always feels the direction of the healing energy as it passes through or around them, and the person receiving the healing energy also feels the sensation of the energy entering their physical body.

Another experiment that has always fascinated me is feeling the energy of the guide when asked to come forward to blend with their medium. When conducting this exercise, I will pick a group member to come forward and sit in the middle of the circle. I will then ask for that group member to go through the process of beginning to blend into the altered state. I will then request that the guide who is beginning to blend with that medium make the contact and to stand behind the medium sitting on the chair.

At this point, I will call on other members of the circle to come forward, one at a time, and put their hand in a controlled manner into the energy of the guide who is standing behind the medium. After they have done this, I will then ask for them to take their hand away from the energy of the guide and get them to raise their hand above the energy of the guide and to slowly bring down their hand to see if they can feel where the guide's energy starts, and then ask them to follow the shape of the energy of the guide standing behind the medium.

I find that this type of exercise gives the group members the understanding that, when we are dealing with our guides, the energy that they bring forward to us has form and is alive. I will never conduct these exercises with any group or individual person without the consent of the guides.

This exercise must never be experimented with any medium in an altered state of trance without the guides' permission. Touching uninvited into the energy created between the guides and the medium when blended in the altered state of trance without the consent of the guides can have a detrimental effect on the health of the medium.

Hot Hands

I have always had the feeling of hot hands when I've been involved in the energy of the spirit world. I found out very early in my development that, when I am in the company of others, my hands would start to become hot when around them. I always took this as an indication that someone around me was requiring a healing.

I was at a workshop and was asked to give a healing to a member of the group. I remember my hands becoming hot before I started to blend with the energy of the healing guide and, after I came out of the altered state, my hands felt oily to the touch. This was something new that had changed with me after that healing session. My hands still secrete an oily substance from time to time after a healing has taken place.

The heating up of hands is quite common amongst healers, but what happened next was a little different. I was lying upon my bed after sitting in the blending process for development when, all of a sudden, my hands started to get hotter and hotter, to the extent it was starting to get uncomfortable. A couple of hours passed and I just lay with my hands down at the side of my body. My hands continued to get hotter and hotter but, by now, the heat had travelled up my arms. It was starting to cause me concern as the heat was now unbearable.

I rose from the bed and went into the bathroom where I ran cold water into the sink. I put both of my hands into the cold water. I was starting to think that I may be experiencing human combustion! I constantly put my hands in and out of the water for about an hour, but the heat did not subside.

I returned back to my bedroom and lay upon the bed with my hands down by my sides. The heat did not subside. I kept asking the spirit world to explain what was happening to me. I heard nothing from them. This heat was increasing and, once again, I headed back to the bathroom to dip my hands back into cold water. I really was getting worried.

I returned back to my bedroom once more and lay upon the bed. I tried to put my mind as far away from the burning feeling as I possibly could. This burning sensation had now travelled from my arms and into my body; it felt like I was suffering from a fever. I just lay there trying to get control of what was happening to me. My body was tingling all over from the heat.

The strange burning sensation lasted through the night and into the following day, and then it started to subside and, eventually, it left. I was relieved but I was never given an explanation as to why it had taken place. Similar burning feelings in my hands and body have occurred a few times through my trance development. I now just accept it when it takes place and trust that there is a reason for it.

Another sensation that can take place within the energy of mediumship is that your fingers can start to swell. I often experience this and always take my rings off when going to do a healing with anyone.

Working With The Public

Up until this point, I had still been working with family and friends in the comfort of my own home, and I thought to myself it was time for me to start looking at opening my own healing clinic.

I decided to take the gamble and to open a healing clinic, one day a month, in a town called Johnstone having created a small bit of interest regarding this type of healing after having a successful demonstration of trance healing in the area.

I will always remember the excitement of arranging the clinic and attending the first day with my wife. I remember the venue I had booked. It was in a room inside a working men's club. The room was dark and dingy, stunk of beer and was riddled with dampness. What a combination! Nothing, however, was going to deter me from trying.

I advertised the clinic for weeks and had four people booked in for a healing appointment on the first day. The next month, I had three booked for a healing and the month after that, I had six.

I never gave up. I was so happy to be given the opportunity to help anyone who would turn up looking for healing. Needless to say, the clinic is still going from strength to strength today. I'm delighted to report that it is no longer in the room stinking of drink and dampness.

I had no idea that this clinic was going to be so important in my journey, not just with helping people with conditions and ailments but that the spirit world would use it for a platform for them to experiment with me.

I had a gentleman who came to visit my clinic who had an addiction to cocaine. The man came into the room, and then made an excuse and proceeded to go to the toilet. When he returned, his pupils where enlarged and he was acting like a different person. I remember speaking to my guide and asking what I should do with him. My initial thought was to ask him to leave but my guide told me to ask him to lie on the healing bed.

I remember the gentleman getting on the bed and asking him to take in three deep breaths. As soon as this was done, I put my hands onto his head, and about three seconds later, he was sound asleep. He was snoring like a bear! I never moved my hands from holding his head and, when he awoke after the healing session, his mannerisms were back to normal. I never saw this gentleman again but did have contact with his mother from time to time. She claimed that he was no longer involved with that substance anymore. We must trust what our guides say to us for we are working together as a team.

I had a lady who came to the clinic who was trying to conceive a child. The lady had travelled the path, as many do, down the route of IVF which had been unsuccessful on a few occasions for her and her husband. This was the first client I had worked with who was asking to see what the spirit world could do to help her with this situation regarding infertility issues.

I asked the lady to lie on the healing bed and proceed to take in three deep breaths. I felt the energy of the person from spirit blend into my energy and then I gently laid my hands onto her head. A short time passed and I felt the energy around me begin to change. I felt my body rise from the chair and I proceeded to move down the bed to the general area of her womb.

I felt my hands move to a position so that they were hovering about 18 inches above her physical body. I was aware of what felt like electricity surging through my hands and entering into her spirit body, which had risen about twelve inches above her physical body. The transference of this surging energy took place for approximately five or six minutes.

I then felt the energy that was around me change once again and, in my mind's eye, I was aware of a tray of spiritual surgical instruments that had appeared to the side of my physical body.

The person who was working through me picked up a cloth from the tray, dipped it into a solution and wiped over the general area of the spiritual womb of the lady.

As the spirit surgeon began to work, a spiritual instrument was lifted from the tray and an incision was made into the womb area. A clamp was used to separate the incision that had been made. The surgeon then lifted up a couple of instruments from the tray and delicately placed them inside where the incision had been made. I was shown that they were working on the spiritual ovary and the fallopian tube.

The surgeon was picking up and placing instruments back onto the tray, selecting what was required before proceeding with his work. He seemed to use an instrument that went inside the fallopian tube. He pushed something at the top of the instrument he had selected and then he slowly retracted it back out as if it was scraping or cleaning inside. He then proceeded to pick up another strange-looking instrument and wash down the area he had been working on. Then it appeared that there was some stitching taking place internally. The clamps were removed and there seemed to be more sewing as if to close up where the incision had been made and then, once more, a solution was wiped over the area with a cloth.

I felt the energy changing around me and, once again, I was standing with my hands hovering above the womb area of the lady. I was aware of a red-coloured energy that was emanating through my hands, and I was shown in my mind that this red healing energy was filling up the lady's womb. A short time later, I felt the energy of the trance blending starting to leave me. I stood at the side of the bed for a few minutes contemplating what had just happened. I let the lady sleep for a few minutes before gently waking her up.

The lady got in touch about eight weeks later to arrange another appointment for a follow-up healing and to share with me her wonderful news that she was with child. I was delighted to hear her exciting news but I was unable to offer her another appointment at that time. As a rule, I do not work with women who are going through the joyous celebration of pregnancy unless they have become aware that there is a complication with the child in the womb.

The lady gave birth to a beautiful baby girl, and she brought her daughter along to the clinic so my wife, Gail, and I could meet her. I felt truly humbled and privileged to have been part of this joyous event.

A lady came along to see me who had problems with her knees. She had been struggling with pain in her knees for many months and had made an appointment to attend at the healing clinic.

The lady arrived at the clinic and she divulged that her knees were feeling like they were beginning to seize up. The lady was in a lot of pain when standing and walking. She went on to explain that she had been a keen keep-fit fanatic all her life and enjoyed jogging as a pastime but, sadly, the pain had become too much for her to continue with any kind of exercise.

I asked her to lie upon the healing bed, and I went to my usual starting position at the end of the bed where her head lay. I went into the altered state and felt the blending take place.

After a short period of time had elapsed, I felt myself rising up from the seat and moving down the bed towards the direction of the lady's knees.

When I reached the area of the lady's knees, I felt the blending of the energy change again and I became aware in my mind that another spirit gentleman was standing at the other side of the bed watching the proceedings. The gentleman, who was now working through me, was not the same person who blended with me at the beginning when I was sitting at the end of the bed.

This was someone new who had come forward to work through me. I suppose, in hindsight, he was a knee specialist. All of a sudden, once again, I found myself to be standing alongside my own physical body and I was looking at myself. Even today when this occurs from time to time, I still find it intriguing.

The gentleman who was working through me proceeded to take an instrument from the tray that had appeared next to me and he made a large incision over the spiritual kneecap. He then proceeded to cut around the bone of the knee and then remove the top of the knee and lay it on a tray. Then he put down the instrument he was using and lifted up another couple of instruments and removed some small pieces of cartilage or bone from within the knee.

The spirit knee surgeon then picked up a file and he scraped at the bone inside the kneecap as if he were reshaping things. He then proceeded to put things back together inside the knee.

He was shaping and cleaning each part before delicately placing it back where it came from. When the internal surgery was complete, he set the top of the kneecap back in its proper place.

He then picked up what appeared to be a cylinder-shaped tube and sealed the top of the kneecap with a solution that was being squeezed from it. The solution was squirted all the way around the knee area before the skin was pulled back over the kneecap. I watched as the surgeon sewed up the incision that had been made. I could see my physical body being shuffled around the bed to the other side of the lady and the same procedure took place with the other knee.

When the spirit surgeons were finished, I felt myself returning back into my physical body through the energy of the blending and, after a few minutes, I was back within the healing room.

The lady reported a few months later that the problem with her knees did not recur after the healing.

My father-in-law had also been suffering with a sore knee. He has got to be one of the most sceptical people I know. He had been limping for a few weeks with severe pain in his knee. He had come along for a visit at my home and I offered to see what the spirit surgeons could do to help him. We were sitting on my couch, and I lifted his sore leg up and placed it so it was lying over my own legs. I then asked him to close his eyes and take in three deep breaths.

I felt the blending of spirit energy take hold of my energy and, very quickly, I became aware of his spirit leg rising above his physical leg. The person working through me picked up a spirit instrument and made an incision on his spiritual knee and pulled back the skin. He then used another instrument and made an incision around the kneecap freeing the knee from the joint. Another medical tool was lifted from the tray of instruments that appeared to be put between the knee joint and used to separate the kneecap. The spirit surgeon picked up various instruments that looked like files and shaped tools to scrape the bone and reshape the knee joint.

At one stage of the proceedings, there was what looked like a hammer that was being used to tap the end of one of the spirit instruments that was being used when reshaping the knee joint. After the spirit surgeon was finished with the scraping and filling, he removed the instrument that separated the knee joint and lowered the knee back onto the joint.

Once again, there was a cylindrical tube that was lifted from the tray and squeezed to release a solution that was put around the knee joint to seal it. The spiritual skin was pushed back together, and this time the skin was joined together with an instrument that looked like it was used to staple the skin back together. His spiritual leg was then lowered back into his physical leg.

As the spirit surgeon had completed his work, I felt the energy of the blending retract from me and, after a few minutes, I had returned back to my father-in-law staring at me in disbelief! He proceeded to tell me that he had his eyes closed, and had become aware of something tapping upon his knee and believed that I was tapping something against it while his eyes were closed.

To his disbelief, when he opened his eyes, he found that I was working about a foot in height above his knee with no contact to his physical body but he could feel the tapping taking place. He still talks about his experience which completely astounded him that day and loves to tell people that he has never had a problem with his knee since.

This was a whole different kind of experience from the last time that I had worked on the lady with the sore knees. This time I was not standing outside my physical body. I was contained within the blending energy of my own physical body and being shown the proceedings of what was taking place through pictures in my mind.

A lady got in touch and made an appointment to visit my clinic. Her name was Pat and she had been diagnosed with terminal cancer of the oesophagus. The Doctors at Pat's hospital had given her a timescale of between six and 18 months to live.

Pat arrived at the healing clinic in Edinburgh and, within 15 minutes, I knew everything about her life. She is a lovely person who has the ability to light up a room when she enters, and can talk the hind legs off a donkey!

Pat explained that she had read an article about me in a newspaper and that article had prompted her to get in touch for a healing. She said she had nothing to lose and had organised a friend to bring her through to Edinburgh.

Two hours had passed and I still had not managed to get Pat onto the healing bed as she was holding conversation after conversation. Pat divulged that she was refusing to take anymore chemo as the hospital had managed to overdose her system causing horrific side effects.

I managed to suggest (after about three hours) that, if it was OK with her, then we would commence with the healing. Pat lay upon the healing bed and I proceeded to go into an altered state. I felt the blending take place with my healing guide, and my hands rising up after a few minutes and touching onto the sides of her head.

A short period of time passed and then I felt my physical body rise from the seat and move round so that I was standing at the side of the healing bed with my hands hovering roughly about 18 inches above Pat's chest area.

The blending with this guide started to change and I felt another guide's energy coming forward to work. I was observing the proceedings that were taking place, not by standing alongside my physical body this time, I was actually watching everything that was taking place through the strangest feeling of being inside my own eye sockets looking out through the guide's eyes.

I watched as the spirit body of Pat rose above her physical body, and the surgeon working through me reached for a cloth dipped in a solution and started to wipe over the chest area of the spirit body of Pat. I could see a nurse who had wheeled in a tray of spiritual instruments standing opposite me and then I watched as the surgeon picked up a spiritual scalpel and made an incision into the spiritual chest of Pat.

I watched in amazement as the surgeon picked up instrument after instrument and proceeded to work within the spiritual chest. The whole operation lasted for approximately 20 minutes, then the surgeon stitched up the incision that had been made in the spiritual chest of Pat.

There was another shift in the energy and another healing guide stepped into my energy. This healer hovered my hands above the area that the work had been carried out on (Pat's chest area) for about five minutes. I then felt the energy retract from me and, within a few minutes, I was back in control of my own body. I asked Pat to gently bring her awareness back into the room.

It was a few minutes before Pat explained that she had had the strangest of experiences when the healing was taking place. She had felt that there were hands moving about inside her physical chest.

Pat stayed for another half an hour or so before saying her goodbyes. I did feel sorry for the person who was sitting outside waiting for her in the car as Pat had stayed for four and a half hours for a half hour appointment!

Pat attended all her future hospital appointments and refused any type of treatment from them. She was given the all-clear with her condition after five years and is living life to the full today.

Pat would like me to mention that she had informed the consultants at the hospital that she believes that the spirit world played a major part in her wonderful results. Pat commented that, when she was attending a follow-up appointment, one of the consultants said to her that if they took cancer themselves, then they would be making a visit to see her healing man!

As a healer, I never claim to be able to cure any ailment or disease. I'm only a vessel for the energy to be channelled through but it is lovely for people to acknowledge the hard work that the spirit world do for us, when they are asked to help with matters that cause us concern.

Reading The Auric Field

The auric field is our life force energy that surrounds our physical body. The energy that emanates through it has the ability to generate colour within it, and many mediums can read information from it. I have found that, when you feel or look into the energy of the aura, the colours that can be perceived can change with health or mood. I think it is important to remember that not all people read colour the same way and you should go with what feels right to you, when you see or feel different colours.

I was sitting one afternoon at my healing clinic speaking to a client. When, all of a sudden, the energy around the lady's auric field started to expand outwards. I watched with great intrigue as I was not trying to work within the energy of the lady's aura. Then, to my surprise, I became aware of words appearing within the energy of the lady's aura.

It was like looking at a computer print-out of her life; it continued to scroll down more and more as I attempted to read what I was seeing. This took place for around five minutes; and then the energy around the lady retracted and the words were no longer visible to me. I was in awe of what had just happened. I had often heard mediums talking about the information contained within the auric field but to be shown it that way was mind-blowing!

It has never been shown to me that way again but the possibilities are always there. It is all about us trusting and allowing them to experiment with us, to enhance our understanding of our mediumistic journey.

Strange Case — Gentleman With Crackling Noise In His Mouth

A young man got in touch with an ailment that was driving him to despair. He had visited the dentist for some work to be carried out and, after the dentist injected his gum with anaesthetic, a continuous crackling noise started in his throat and mouth area. The young man was at his wits' end with the noise as it was affecting his sleep and general well-being. He had travelled to America to visit a private specialist at his own expense and found no solution to the problem.

I asked the young man to lie upon the healing bed and I went into the altered state. A few minutes had passed within the blending with my guide, and I felt my hands being lifted onto the throat area of the young man. I could feel a buzz of energy flowing through my hands and into the gentleman. The crackling noise stopped and then restarted. The process of the noise stopping and starting continued for the duration of the healing under the control of the healer working through me.

I felt the energy once again retract from the blending process with my healing guide, and asked the young man to gently bring himself back. The crackling noise was still present with the young man but the noise was softer. The young man returned for another four appointments before the noise completely subsided and he could eventually return back to a normal life.

When the first healing had taken place with the young man and the crackling noise was softer in volume, I knew then that the energy the spirit healer was controlling through my hands had the ability to help the young man with his condition. If they were able to stop and start the noise then they would be able to control it through time.

Lady With Growth In The Brain

I was working in Glasgow with a lady who had a 28 millimetre growth in the front of her brain. The growth was in such a place that it was causing the lady to have severe head pain, and she had been informed by the hospital that it was inoperable.

The hospital was monitoring it closely and had advised the lady that there was a possibility that she may end up in a wheelchair. The specialist at the hospital suggested that they would like to proceed with radiotherapy treatment. This type of treatment can stop the growth from becoming larger and can shrink it by a few millimetres in size. The lady had a young family and, as she spoke about her condition, my heart went out to her.

I asked the lady to lie upon the healing bed and to relax after taking in three deep breaths. I quickly went into the altered state and, after the blending with my guide was complete, I felt my hands being lifted onto the lady's head. My hands did not move from the area of her head.

The energy just flowed through my hands under the control of the healing guide.

When the healing with the lady was finished, I felt the energy of the guide leave me and I returned back from the blending process. When the lady returned to full consciousness, she stated that she did not have any pain in her head. The lady booked another appointment and left.

When the lady arrived for her second appointment, she revealed that she had not had a sore head for a month. She also mentioned that she had been in to speak with her consultant and the radiotherapy treatment was scheduled in a week's time. The lady had a few more appointments at the healing clinic over the months before going to the hospital for a scan.

The lady got in touch after she had the scan results and shared the wonderful news that the growth had shrunk down by half: it now measured 14 millimetres! She also announced that the specialist had said he was lost for words!

The good news did not stop there. The lady continued to attend my healing clinic over the next year. She had no more radiotherapy treatment at the hospital and, when she had her last scan, the growth had completely gone!

We do not have control of the outcome of any healing that takes place. We can only offer ourselves of service to the spirit world and be the best channel for them to work through us. The results are out of our control. The healing energy comes from their side of life and mixes with our energy creating a working partnership between the two energies.

The Transition

This is a topic that took me some time to understand. I always want the best results for anyone who comes seeking help from the spirit world. I thought that a healer's job was always to heal but sometimes it's about understanding what the healing is all about.

I got a call from a lady who asked if I could do a home visit to her mother who was terminally ill with ovarian cancer. I arrived at the house and the lady was too frail for me to get her to lie upon the portable healing bed. I went into the lady's bedroom with the permission from her daughter and got the frail lady to lie upon her own bed.

I went into the blending process and worked with the lady for about half an hour under the watchful eye of an observer who I always have with me when any healing is taking place. When the healing had finished, I left the lady sleeping on her bed and said my goodbyes to her daughter.

About a week later, I received a lovely email from the lady's daughter explaining that after the healing, her mother was at peace with her condition and was ready to let go, and had returned back to heaven.

I was sad with hearing this news about the lady but, on the other hand, I was glad in a caring way that the healing had worked. It would be true to say I initially had wanted the spirit world to heal her from the cancerous condition, but the healing energy had connected her back into the love of the spirit world and the lady was now at peace.

I just did not realise at that time in my spiritual journey, until speaking with Henry, that there was more to the workings of the spirit world than me just wanting them to help rectify problems and ailments that lie within the physical body.

When it is time for the spirit to return back into the love of the spirit world, one of the jobs of a healer is to allow the spirit guides to connect the spirit back into the energy of heaven.

I went to a hospice to visit my uncle who had been living with a terminal condition and had fought bravely right up to his transition.

When I arrived at the hospice and sat alongside my uncle at his bed, I became aware of family members from the spirit side of life who were gathering around him within the room. I knew then that they were not there to bring healing to him, they were assembling to meet and greet him when the time was right for them to collect him.

I asked my aunt if it was OK for me to place my hands onto my uncle's head and give him a healing. My aunt agreed. I put my right hand on his head and the other hand onto his chest over his heart area. I then went into an altered state. What happened next was a new experience for me.

I heard Henry telling me to just relax and let the energy connect with my uncle. I was glad to hear the comforting words from Henry as I was emotional, knowing my uncle was not for this world much longer.

I became aware of an immense white light that shone into my eyes. The light seemed to connect into the energy of my uncle. It felt as if there was a bubble of white light that had connected between us. After about ten minutes of being aware of the white bubble of light, the light started to diminish and I started to return my consciousness back into the room. I knew then that the healing that had taken place was about the connection of his spirit back into the spirit world.

It was a privilege and an honour to be given the opportunity to connect my uncle back into the love of the spirit world. My uncle sadly passed over a few days later but it was comforting to know that he was no longer in pain and his transition back into heaven was peaceful.

Healing Thoughts

A lady got in touch about her mother. Her mum had been unwell over a long period of time with her condition. The lady had been asking for distant healing to be sent for her mother and lots of people had been involved sending healing at her request.

The lady was heartbroken at the thought of her mum passing over but she knew that her mother would not recover from her condition. The thought of her mother still being here and suffering in pain was causing distress in the family.

The lady asked through a barrage of tears if there was anything that could be done to ease her mother's pain. The lady explained that seeing her mum like this was breaking her heart.

I explained that, when we ask for healing to be sent to someone, those in the spirit world will bring that energy forward to connect with the spirit of the person (in this case her mother) that the healing has been asked for.

When the spirit energy has been brought forward, the intention set behind what has been asked is for the energy to heal. This means that the energy requested will rejuvenate or give a boost to the spirit of the person that the healing request has been asked for, and will continue until the spirit is ready to return back into heaven.

I suggested that all the healing energy that had been requested for her mother be changed to the thought of getting her ready for her transition back into the spirit world. The lady did this and her mother passed over peacefully a few days later when she was ready.

Spirit Technology

Those who live in the spirit world do not sit idly by waiting for us to get in touch. They are constantly working at 100 miles an hour looking at, developing and teaching each other and us new ways to do things.

I was working in one of my clinics with a gentleman who had a stomach complaint. I asked the gentleman to lie upon the healing bed and I went into the blending process. A few minutes had passed when I felt myself being lifted-up from the chair and moved to the side of the healing bed. My eyes were fully closed at this time and had been with every healing that had taken place on my healing journey.

When they lift me up from a chair or shuffle me around a

healing bed, my eyes are always fully closed. When I was at the side of the healing bed, I became aware of lots of spirit people assembling in the room. I felt the blend of energy starting to change with the guide working through me and another guide coming forward.

When this new guide came forward, he proceeded to pick up an instrument with what looked like a flex attached to it and connect it onto my right eye. I felt my hands reach forward and pick up what I can only explain as two pairs of handles that you would find on the end of scissors with rods attached to them.

The spirit surgeon was looking down through the contraption attached to my right eye and was operating inside the spirit stomach of the gentleman with these scissor-looking handles attached to the rods that appeared to be inside the spirit body. I watched in amazement as the spirit surgeon was working away with the instruments in his hands. It was like looking at the very first type of keyhole surgery.

I observed as the surgeon finished his work and then disconnected the instrument from my eye. I felt the energy of the blending starting to retract and, within a few minutes, I was fully back. I then asked the client to gently come back as the healing was finished. What had taken place with this healing was truly bizarre as the instruments used were crude in their appearance but I'm sure they were ground-breaking in their time.

About six months later, I was working at the same clinic with a lady who had a stomach complaint. The lady got onto the healing bed and I went into the blending process. I felt the energy of the guide come forward and, after a few minutes, I found myself standing at the side of the healing bed. I was not in my physical body; I was standing alongside my own physical body watching myself being controlled by the spirit surgeon.

My attention was drawn so that I was looking at a monitor that was floating above the bed and the surgeon standing alongside me was holding in his hands instruments that were attached with rods. The rods were attached inside the spiritual body of the lady who was floating above her physical body.

I watched the surgeon carry out an operation with a different method of keyhole surgery. This time the instruments and proceedings were more modern in appearance. The vision of what I had been watching started to disappear into the vibration of the energy as I felt myself merging back into my physical body and, after a few minutes, I was back.

The most important thing to remember about these two similar surgeries is the understanding that those from the spirit side of life use different types of technology depending on what time of history they work from.

Teaching Spirit To Heal

I was working with a lady who had a heart condition. I had blended with a guide and found myself, once again, standing outside my physical body. I watched as the guide controlling my body hovered my hands over the area of the lady's heart for quite some time.

There was another older-looking spirit gentleman standing alongside me, observing what was taking place and also about another ten or twelve spirit people standing around the vicinity of the healing bed. I watched as the spirit gentleman who was controlling my physical body moved back to the end of the healing bed and sat back on the chair.

I then saw the energy of the healer move out of my physical body, and the older gentleman standing alongside me merged into my physical body. The older gentleman rose my physical body from the chair, leaned over the lady's head and proceeded to examine the work that had been done with the previous gentleman who had blended with me.

I became aware of words being spoken between them and then they changed positions within my physical body. The first gentleman rose my physical body from the seat and moved round the side of the healing bed. I watched as he lifted my hands over the area of the lady's spirit heart once again and, after a few minutes, he returned my physical body back to the chair.

The older gentleman, once again, stepped forward and blended into my vibration, had a look at what had been corrected by the first gentleman, and I then felt my own energy returning back into my physical body.

This was the first time I had become aware that, when a healing takes place, there are people from the spirit side of life who could be given the opportunity to learn how to heal through people like me who have dedicated their lives to be of service to the divine creator.

A Young Boy Who Would Not Settle

A lady brought her young son to visit one of my healing clinics. He was suffering with a heart murmur. I got the young boy to lie upon the healing bed, and I proceeded to go into the blending with my guide. The young boy would not settle. He was wriggling all over the bed, kicking his legs outwards and, at one point, singing to himself!

I found myself speaking to Henry when the healing was taking place and asked him if we should stop. Henry said everything would be OK, and lifted my right physical hand with my thumb raised and gently flicked my thumb onto the little boy's forehead.

The little boy instantly fell asleep and I heard Henry say to the mother, "You won't get that on the NHS!" The little boy did not reawaken until the healing was completed.

Trance Healing

Trance healing is the purest type of spiritual healing when developed properly. It takes years and years of sitting and blending with your healing guides to get the connection and control with them correct.

You must allow your guides, who come to work through you, to have complete control over the flow of the healing energy through the blending process with you and not have your own thoughts drift into the healing.

If your thoughts encroach on the process of the healing that is taking place, then the flow of energy and the control that the healing guide needs is being interfered with by you. It takes time to learn not to bring your thoughts into the healing process.

The simplest of thoughts can interfere. The desire to help the client and asking the guide to do his or her best should always be done before the healing begins, and not in the middle of the healing when it is taking place.

You must always remember that you cannot heal any disease or ailment. You are only the channel for the healing energy to be administered through by the direction and control of your healing guide when blending with you.

Trance healing is a wonderful gift which has been given to us from the spirit world and, as with all types of spiritual healing, should never be taken lightly. When you go down the path of healing mediumship, you are offering yourself to be of service to the divine creator. You are also building lasting friendships and trust with those who come forward to work through you from the spirit side of life. The healing guides who work with you have also offered themselves of service and have chosen to work with you.

How Trance Healing Works

The mechanics for trance healing blending is no different to trance mediumship. The blending of energies is the same procedure only this time, when a healing is going to take place, we set our intention at the beginning that we are asking for healers to come forward from spirit and blend into our vibration.

There is a team of healers and helpers who gather from the spirit side of life to participate in the proceedings of the healing that is going to take place under the direction of your main healing guide. Your main healing guide is in charge of the whole procedure within the structure of the healing process.

There is always a discussion amongst the spirit healers as to the best course of action to proceed with the healing. We, as the vessel, are not usually privileged to be included in this conversation. The reason for this is that we may try to influence the outcome of the healing by bringing our own thoughts into our minds regarding what we have previously overheard them discuss about the client.

When the spirit healers have their discussion at the beginning of the healing, they are looking at the best way to proceed with the healing energy that is required for the client. All healing energy is transferred through vibration in colour.

Hypothetically, if a client comes regarding a kidney concern, the spirit healers and guides may decide that orange healing energy is required for that condition and, if another condition is detected with the spirit body of the client, let's say a pancreas complaint, then they may introduce the healing energy in the colour yellow for that condition. This is why a client may make a comment after a healing that they were aware of colours appearing in their mind's eye throughout the healing.

There is always an alchemist who is part of your healing team. The job of the alchemist is to mix the healing colours required within the healing process and to administer them into the vibration of the energy created between the spirit healer and the healing medium who are working and blending their energies together in the altered state of trance. This is where trance healing is a little bit different to other types of spiritual healing.

Let me quickly explain the workings of a spiritual healing medium. With the act of spiritual healing, the healing medium opens themselves up to the energy of the spirit world or the universal energy. They offer themselves to be of service to allow the healing energy to flow through them.

The healing medium, in essence, becomes a conduit for the healing energy to enter into them and pass out through them. The healer does not have any control within the direction of the flow of energy that travels within the spiritual body of the client.

The spiritual healing energy that travels in and out through the healing medium has an intelligence behind it. It travels and searches through the spiritual body within the physical body of the client with the intention to seek out ailments that lie within and to heal.

Spiritual healing is about being the best vessel that you can be. To let the healing energy pass through you to help people who seek help with their ailments or conditions that are or have been causing them concern. I hope that quickly covers the workings of spiritual healing.

Now back to trance healing.

When the blending with the healing guide and healing medium is complete, the alchemist then introduces the healing colours, that were mixed together at the beginning of the healing, into the vibration of the blended energies between the spirit healer and the healing medium.

The healing energy with the colour is administrated through the direction of the trance healing guide and the controlled flow of energy travels directly to the part of the spiritual body that is causing the client concern within their physical body.

Trance healing energy that is administered does not have to search through the spiritual body of the client. It travels directly through the guidance and control of the healing guide to the area that has been giving concern to the client.

The spiritual energy used with both types of healing are exactly the same. There cannot be any difference with the source of the healing energy because the energy can only come from one source known as the spirit world, universal energy or the divine creator. It must be noted, however, that different cultures have different terms for the same source.

The only difference is the way the energy is being utilised through the vibration for the purpose of healing. One type of healing energy (spiritual healing) seeks and searches, and the other (trance) is administered and controlled directly through a healing guide who has blended with a trance healing medium to the area of the spirit body that is causing concern.

The healing energy does not stop when the healing has finished. The healing energy continues to work on the client for as long as it is required. The job of the healer is to make contact with the spirit of the client to establish the connection on behalf of the spirit world.

I am always asking my guides how things work within the healing energy, and I thought their explanation about vibrational healing was wonderful. We live in vibrational worlds.

Everything that you feel, see and hear in your world is a vibration. Everything breaks down into atoms, matter and protons.

The human body is a vibration, and every internal organ inside resonates at a separate vibrational frequency. When the vibration is not correct then that internal part of the human anatomy is not working properly allowing disease and complications to arise.

I was given an analogy from spirit: When a clock has a

pendulum and something goes wrong with the mechanical workings within the clock, the pendulum can start to run faster or become slower causing a problem with the mechanism of the clock. When the internal workings of the clock have been corrected then the pendulum will move back to the proper frequency and the workings of the clock will return back to normal.

The healing colour is administered through the vibration of the healing energy that has been connected into the vibration of the spirit body and, in due course, transferred into the physical body of the client with the intention to help with any ailment or condition the client is having concerns with. The most important thing to remember is that, every time a healing takes place, it is an experiment and no guarantee is ever given.

The healing process is not as simple as putting your hands on or above the client and asking for help. There is a multitude of spirit people involved in a spiritual healing. It starts with the client searching for help and them being guided in the right direction from higher powers to the right healer on our side of life who the spirit world believe is best suited for the healing to help that particular person at that time.

When a healing takes place, the alchemist who is present is being given instructions to mix the colours required. The alchemist mixes the colours under the direction of the healing guides who have discussed the case at the spirit consultation.

There is your doorkeeper/protector and their job is to allow the energy of any guide who is compatible with your energy to come forward and work through you. Then there will be another guide who will come forward and blend within your energy, and their job is to check that all is well with you and the client to allow the healing to proceed. This guide is usually a psychologist.

There will be another healing guide who will come forward and blend with your energy. The job of this healing guide is to allow the healing energy blended together from the alchemist to mix with your energy, creating a bubble of energy around the client and yourself for protection.

The bubble of energy, that has been created through the blending process, enables the medium to become a generator of trance vibrational energy, allowing other guides and spirit workers to connect into the energy created around the bed.

The healing guide working through the medium will administer the healing energy into the spirit body of the client and, if required, will allow himself or herself to change positions within the blending process with other healing guides at any time through the whole procedure.

There will be a multitude of spirit healers working directly through the medium when a healing is taking place within the bubble of energy that has been created through the connection with you, the healing medium, the client and the spirit world. This bubble of energy also allows other teams of spirit workers to work upon the client as well.

Near the end of the healing, another guide will come forward and blend with your energy. This guide will oversee what has been done within the spirit body of the client. This is usually carried out under the control of your main guide, in my case Henry.

This is how a trance healing works with you and your healing guides who come forward to work through you when a healing has been requested. Trance healing is a progressive type of healing, the more you trust the guides who work through you, the less involvement you will have in what can be achieved.

The more we allow our minds to be involved in the procedure, the less control the healing guides have over us and the blending of the energy to carry out the wonderful work that they can do through us. Remember to keep your thoughts out of what is taking place.

I remember asking my guides at a clinic after a young man arrived with a blood disorder: "How are you going to work with this man's condition?" The answer I received was to observe what takes place.

The young man got onto the healing bed and I went into the blending process. A few minutes passed and I felt my physical body being lifted from the seat and moved to the bottom of the gentleman's lower right leg.

I was observing the proceedings from the left side of my physical body that was being controlled through the healing guide. I watched as the guide lifted my hands and placed them around the lower right leg of the young man. I became aware of a shimmering energy that contained colour expand through and around the area of the young man's leg.

The energy surrounding the young man's right lower leg grew under the control of the healing guide. The energy remained there for about five minutes and then started to diminish until it appeared that it was just my hands, with no energy around them, that were wrapped around the young man's right leg.

I felt the energy of the blending start to leave and I was being drawn back into my physical body. After a few minutes, I was back and out of the altered state. I then heard Henry's voice saying: "We cannot operate on blood, so we have to build an energy screen allowing the blood to pass through the vibration of the screen to cleanse it."

This made complete sense to me and gave more of an understanding that those from the spirit side of life always know what the best plan of attack is when a healing has been requested by a person in distress.

I had a lady who arrived for a healing who was suffering with fibromyalgia. The lady had been very active in her life but, over a period of a few years, the pain had increased so much that her quality of life had diminished.

I went into the blending process and, once again after a few minutes, I felt my physical body being lifted from my position at the end of the healing bed. My hands were raised and brought down to touch the right side of the lady's head.

My body was then moved round to the right side of the lady who was lying upon the healing bed. I became aware that my hands were being carefully placed onto different parts of the lady's body. The guide paid particular attention to the back of the lady's hands before moving onto her hip area, and then down the length of her right leg and onto her right foot. The guide moved my hands across onto the lady's left foot and carried out the same procedure of laying my hands up the left side of the lady's body until I was back at the top of the healing bed, where I had started the blending process.

When the healing was finished, the lady mentioned that she had experienced a sensation of immense heat that had filled her whole body, and that she had the feeling of pins and needles all over.

I heard back from the lady a few days later. She revealed that she had felt like her old self once again. She had no pain and had gone out dancing on the evening after the healing. I was delighted to hear that wonderful news.

Fibromyalgia is a very painful condition that affects many people in the world today. It is comforting to know that I have worked with lots of clients with this condition and always have had positive feedback.

Eyes Closed

I had been working for many years in the altered state of trance within the field of healing and had always had my eyes closed when working. I suppose there is no need for your eyes to be open as you are developing to allow your guides to control your physical body through the blending process.

I remember the first time I had the inclination to stand up at a workshop. I started to sway backwards and forwards when in the blended state. I had the feeling, as the momentum started to become stronger for me, to stand up from the chair. My own thoughts of what was happening were interfering with what they were trying to achieve.

I remember getting a lecture from the course organiser at the time about how I was interfering with what they were trying to do with me, and I was not to interfere if it happened again in the next sitting.

The next sitting came and, within a few minutes of the blending, I started to sway once again backwards and forwards in the chair. Once again, the momentum started to become stronger. I felt my arms being lifted and, all of a sudden, I was standing up on my feet with my eyes closed.

I could feel my body swaying from side to side as I stood in front of the chair. I then felt the energy around me as if it was giving direction for me to sit back down. I sat back on the chair, and was quietly chuffed with myself for following the feeling and not interfering this time.

I was in the seat for a few minutes when the swaying motion of moving forward and backwards started again and, within seconds, I was back up standing in front of the chair and then sitting back down.

This motion of standing up and sitting back down on the chair did not stop, and for the next two hourly sessions of sitting with the group, I found myself standing up and sitting down under the direction of the guide working with me.

The following day, like clockwork, I was swaying backwards and forwards as I sat on the chair. Once again, I was standing up in front of the chair but, this time, I did not sit back down. The guide moved me forward a few steps and then shuffled me back to the chair.

This went on for a few hours. Each time the guide would walk me further away from the chair and then shuffle me backwards to the chair. The more the guide did this, the more confident I became with the procedure of walking forward and being brought back to the chair.

The group broke for lunch and, after I had overindulged, I went for a walk to clear my head out of the energy of the blending in the morning session.

We returned back for the afternoon session and, once again, I found myself swaying backwards and forwards on the chair and then standing up from the chair. The guide started to walk me forward, but this time my confidence was high and I took control of the blending process with the guide, and I proceeded to walk straight across the room.

Within the centre of the group was a séance trumpet that had been given to the course organiser by a friend. The trumpet had allegedly belonged to the famous physical medium from Scotland called Helen Duncan.

I walked straight into the path of the séance trumpet and kicked it across the room, just missing one of the group members by inches as it flew past his head when he was sitting in the altered state.

I heard the course organiser's stern voice: "Stop right there and don't move any further! Bring yourself back out of the connection with the energy and return to your seat."

I returned back to my seat with my head hung low. The course organiser said, "I don't need to tell you what went wrong there with the blending." I knew within myself that my eagerness had interfered and I had taken control of the connection with my guide.

Thankfully, the course organiser then said: "The good thing about what you did was that no-one has seen that séance trumpet move in years and I saw it move today with you." This broke the ice and brought a lot of laughter to the room.

The following day the group came together for the morning session and, once again, the swaying motion started when I was sitting in the chair. I was swaying this time from side to side like a pendulum.

The motion of swinging from side to side went on for hours and then it changed, and I started to sway backwards and forwards. The motion of swaying backwards and forwards started to gain momentum and I snapped the back of the chair completely in two parts. I got a hell of a fright when this happened and was jolted out of the blending process.

The course organiser just looked at me and said, "Are you OK?" "Yes," I replied. "OK, then go back into the blending and settle yourself for a few minutes before bringing yourself back."

Later that evening, when on my own, I thought to myself, "Can anything else go wrong? I've only been here two days and already I've almost taken someone's head off its shoulders by kicking the séance trumpet at them, and now I have broken one of the hotel's chairs in half." I just turned off the bedside light and went to sleep.

The following day, the group came together to sit at the morning session and, within a few minutes, I was blended with the energy of my guide and the swaying motion started immediately.

I was swaying backwards and forwards while sitting on the chair. My initial thought was, "Please don't break another chair!" I was then lifted to my feet and was walked a few steps forward but this time the guide did not shuffle me back to the chair. The guide proceeded to turn me around in a complete circle and then shuffled me back to my seat. The procedure of being moved forward, and turned around 360 degrees and returned to my chair continued for the whole morning session.

It takes time to trust your guides and helpers from the spirit side of life, especially when they are lifting you up from sitting in a chair with your eyes closed. When we are in the altered state of trance, there is no reason for our eyes to be open. Our part of the process is to learn to hold their energy within our energy when the blending takes place. The more you sit blending with them, the greater the connection becomes.

The motion of being lifted up from a seat and moved around the room with your eyes closed takes a lot of time and effort from them. It also takes a lot of trust on our part to let ourselves be controlled completely by them.

Eyes Open

Through my healing journey when working with my guides, my eyes were always closed. The guide would raise my physical body up from the chair and shuffle it around the healing bed to work with the spirit of the client, and my eyes would never open. Then one day things changed while working with a client. I heard Henry's voice asking me to open my eyes.

When I heard this, I thought that it was my own imagination interfering with the connection that had been made with my guide.

I heard Henry's voice once again saying, "Open your eyes!" After I heard it a second time, I attempted to open my eyes and found that my eyelids were tightly stuck together. I tried again and, this time, I felt my eyelids starting to free themselves and my eyes were open.

I was blended with my guide with my eyes wide open but I was not looking through my eyes. I was looking through the guide's eyes! It was the strangest feeling. It was as if I was looking out from inside my eye sockets. I was there but I wasn't really there. Everything looked and appeared weird as if I was in amongst the blended energy but not really there.

I watched the guide work with the client with my eyes through his eyes and, after the guide had finished, I felt my eyes close and the blending of our energies start to diminish, and I was back in my own physical body.

This was another truly unique experience for me within the blending process. The process of my eyes being opened within the blending of trance healing with my guides has continued from that day forward.

The feeling of being present and not being present within the blended energy has never changed. The looking out through the guide's eyes also has never changed apart from sometimes experiencing moving from looking out through the guide's eyes to watching the proceedings from the side of my physical body and back to the eyes throughout the duration of a healing.

I have tried many times to try to open my eyes under my own steam when blended with my guides when sitting for trance and physical mediumship. I have never been able to open them or have not been allowed to open them by myself when under the guide's control.

The process of my eyes opening only happens under the control of my guides when a trance healing or psychic surgery is taking place. I have got used to it over the years and don't ever give it a second thought today.

Trance Healing Teaching

I started to teach trance and trance healing by running workshops in the UK, and now have the great honour of holding seminars, workshops and spiritual retreats in various locations across the globe. These teachings and events are always open to all, but I'm afraid that you will not learn to be a trance healer overnight.

Spiritual healing takes an average of two years for you to receive your certificate with all major organisations, and trance healing will take longer to develop. I have mentioned earlier that I developed for four and a half years behind closed doors before I felt confident enough with the spirit world and my healing guides before to taking it out to the public.

Teaching trance healing is a privilege and, as with all types of spiritual development, it should never be taken lightly. There are not enough spiritual healers in the world we live in, and there is enough work for everyone. The procedure with trance healing is the same as with all trance; it's about getting the connection correct with your healing guides.

Trance blending is a development stage of your healing journey, and you must allow them to blend into your energy life force so that they may get control and work upon changing your chemical composition through the blending process.

In the workshops and retreats that I offer for trance development, I make sure that the students' connections with their guides are correct as this builds the foundation for the blending partnership. When the foundation is not correct, the connection will not be stable and then we, as healing mediums, can start to go down the road of pseudo trance.

We, as healing trance mediums, are learning to give ourselves over to the control of the guides, as we are only the vessel or channel for them to work through. The more control they have, the greater the results that will take place through your healing mediumship.

Saying all that, the workshops and retreats are about learning in a safe and comfortable environment with plenty of theory and hands-on practical healing with like-minded people, keeping it simple.

Healing Online

My healing clinics had been growing from strength to strength through word of mouth from my clients. Word of mouth is the best type of promotion that anyone could possibly ask for when working on behalf of the divine source with the spirit world.

I had been asked to do healing over the Internet on many occasions but had never got round to looking at the possibility of using this service with healing. I did not know how to start or if I could develop this particular type of healing with my guides. I decided to sit with Henry to see what came forward.

The advice that came forward from Henry was that in his time things were different from what they are today in our time, and every type of technology must be utilised to aid in the advancement of the understanding of the spirit world.

It had taken me four and a half years of developing behind closed doors before I was happy with the blending with my healing guides and the results that were being achieved with family and friends before I would take it out to the public.

I was in no hurry to start healing over the Internet until it was developed properly with the spirit world. I sent out the invitation to friends and family members to help with developing this type of healing.

It was only a few days later that I found myself sitting in front of my laptop and speaking with a friend after arranging a healing with her. I explained to her that this type of healing was in the infant stage for me, and this was my first attempt so everything would be experimental.

I asked her to close her eyes as I said a prayer for guidance and protection. I then asked her to keep her eyes closed, and to just relax and take in three deep breaths.

When the lady breathed in, I could feel the connection being made with her spirit to my spirit to the spirit world.

I could feel the energy of Henry blending into my energy but I was not in a deep state of trance. I was alert and aware of what was taking place. I could feel the energy of the spirit world all around me in my room. I then became aware that my energy was present within the room that the lady was sitting in. I had become part of the lady's energy within the vibration of the connection made through the energy created with us all through the spirit world.

I watched as the energy in the lady's room appeared to change from physical energy into the vibration of the spirit world energy. When this happened, I could see etheric mist travelling across the lady's room, and I could perceive little spirit lights that would flash around her.

I then became aware of spirit people who appeared in shadow form before showing themselves in a more solid spirit form. I had immense coldness around my legs that felt like an icy breeze. I watched three people from spirit step forward and stand behind the lady. I could also see Henry standing in the middle of the group.

I saw Henry step forward and lift his hands on to either side of the lady's head. A few minutes passed, and then there was an orange glow of energy that appeared around Henry's hands. The orange glow travelled down the head and through the body of the lady until her physical body and head were completely covered in the orange glow.

I watched in amazement as Henry proceeded to lift his hands up, and the spirit of the lady lifted out of her physical body and floated about twelve inches above it. I then saw a spirit surgeon step forward and move to the area of the lady's lower tummy. I then became aware of a spirit nurse appear and push in a tray of spiritual instruments alongside the surgeon.

I watched the spirit surgeon raise her hands, and I could see green energy come out of her hands and into the lower tummy area of the lady's spirit body. I then observed as the surgeon proceeded to pick up one of the spirit instruments and make what looked like an incision into the area of the lady's spirit body that was covered in the green energy.

I became aware of a spirit gentleman who came forward and stood opposite the female surgeon. This spirit gentleman lifted his hands above the spirit body of the lady and, as he hovered his hands over that area, there was a blue energy that started to emanate through his hands and into the spirit body of the lady.

I watched, with great interest, what each spirit person was doing with the healing that was taking place within the spirit body of the lady. I watched as the surgeon continued to carry out the spiritual operation on the area that I thought was the lady's ovary.

The healing continued for about another five minutes. I then became aware of the spirit gentleman, who had been emanating blue energy through his hands, lifting his hands away from the area he had been working on and gently disappeared backwards into the energy in the room. Then the surgeon finished the operation and she gently disappeared into the vibration of the room along with the spiritual instruments.

Henry was still holding onto the spiritual head of the lady, and the colour coming through his hands changed from orange to white. The white light began to glow, and started to travel down the spiritual head and into the spiritual body of the lady changing the colour that was orange into white.

When the spiritual body of the lady was completely engulfed in the colour of white, Henry lowered the spirit body of the lady back into her physical body. He then indicated that I was to inform the lady that she was to relax for a few minutes to allow her spirit to completely return.

Henry disappeared into the vibration in the lady's room, and I watched as the vibration in the room changed from the spirit world to the physical. I waited a few minutes before bringing the lady back. I waited with bated breath to get the lady's feedback on the healing.

The lady said that she could feel the coldness that was all around her. She had become aware of the colour orange, and had felt herself become floaty within the healing. She also mentioned that she could feel her ovary area being worked on and had enjoyed that I had spoken all the way through the healing, explaining what I was aware of taking place. I was so caught up with what was happening that I did not realise I was speaking all the way through it!

The wonderful thing about this healing was that, when the operation was taking place, I could feel slight pain in my own body around the area that was being worked on by the female surgeon on the spirit body of the lady. This experience gave me the understanding that, with this type of healing, there is no distance with the vibration made within the connection to the spirit world.

The second attempt at online healing was with a medium friend. I asked her to take in three deep breaths, and then for her to just relax and concentrate her focus upon her breath. While she had taken in her deep breaths, I had connected with her spirit and the spirit world.

I watched as the vibration of the energy around my friend started to change. There was a blue colour that became visible in her room, then little spirit lights appeared and what looked like clouds of moving mist. Then the coldness arrived in my room. Once again, this coldness was like an icy breeze around my legs.

I observed with interest as the energy building up appeared to pixelate in the room of my friend. I then became aware of three shadow figures standing behind her as she was sitting relaxing on her chair. The energy of the figures became stronger and I became aware of Henry standing behind her.

I watched as Henry stepped closer and put his hands on top of my friend's head, and the colour of green started to emanate through his hands and cover her head. The green-coloured healing energy continued down across her chest and eventually covered her whole body.

I then became aware of the two other shadow people who were standing either side of Henry moving forward to the side of the lady. There was a spirit woman to the lady's left-hand side and a spirit gentleman to her right-hand side.

The spirit woman lifted her hands above the heart area of my friend, and I was watching red energy build up around her hands and entering into the physical body of my friend. The spirit body of my friend did not rise out this time; it remained inside my friend's physical body.

The spirit gentleman who was standing on the right-hand side of my friend put his hands over the eyes of my friend and I was watching yellow energy enter into her eye sockets.

I watched in amazement for about 15 minutes before the spirit woman lifted her hands off the area above my friend's heart and she disappeared back into the vibration of the room. Then the spirit gentleman lifted his hands away from the area of my friend's eyes and he disappeared backwards into the vibration.

When these spirit healers had finished, the colour that they were using to heal did not disappear. The colour appeared to remain on the general area of my friend even though the healers had completed their task.

I then became aware of Henry's hands starting to change colour from green to white. The white energy turned the colour green to white and incorporated the other healing colours, that had been added by the two spirit healers, changing them to white as the energy travelled down through the body of my friend.

When my friend was completely engulfed in white, Henry waited for a few minutes before taking his hands off the head of the lady, and he started to disappear into the vibration of the room. I watched as the room's energy changed from spirit world energy into physical world energy. I waited a few minutes before asking my friend to gently come back.

My friend explained that she was aware of spirit being all around her. She had perceived the colour green and had felt a pressure that was over her eyes. She had also felt the sensation as if someone or something was massaging her heart area. She said that she knew for certain the spirit world was working with her during the session and mentioned that I should be taking healing out to the public.

This was my second online healing and, for me, it was still in the infant stage. The feedback received for both healings was encouraging but it still needed a lot of development before I felt confident enough to take it out to the public.

The next healing was a wonderful experience for me to be part of. Strangely enough, it was with another female friend who was willing to participate with the development of this new type of healing with the spirit world and me.

My friend lay upon her bed in her home and I asked her to take in three deep breaths and then to relax. I waited as the vibration within her room began to change. The energy pixelated and mist started to appear around her.

I was aware of the room becoming purple in colour. As expected, the coldness started around my own legs and I was connected into the energy of her room. I watched as lots of spirit people in shadow form appeared alongside the lady as she lay upon her bed. I observed a figure coming forward and I was aware it was Henry.

Henry put his hands onto the lady's head, and an orange glow appeared around his hands and connected into her head. The orange energy continued to travel down the lady's body until it was completely engulfed within the colour. Henry then proceeded to lift his hands upwards, and the spirit body of the lady floated out of her physical body and hovered under Henry's control about 18 inches above.

I was watching a mirror image of my friend, one a spirit body and the other a physical body, one on top of the other. I then became aware of lots of spirit people who were standing around the bed forming a circle about ten feet away from my friend. To my amazement, I saw lots of spirit children who appeared around the area of the bed and formed an inner circle around my friend.

All the spirit children were emanating a pure white light that glowed from each one. The white light of each joined together and rose above my friend's spiritual body, and then descended into her spiritual body. The spirit people who had formed the outer circle started to emanate a multitude of colours above them, and the colours rose high and then descended and entered into my friend's spiritual body.

I was in awe of what was taking place with this healing for my friend. I had never seen so many spirit people involved in a healing before. The colours that were entering into my friend's spirit body were like looking through the end of a kaleidoscope. They were sparkling and moving as if they had shapes of their own.

I then watched as the spirit people who had formed the outer circle stopped emanating the colours and they all disappeared backwards into the vibration. Then the spirit children stopped emanating their beautiful white colour and stepped back into the vibration.

Henry was left holding his hands onto the head of the lady's spirit head, and then I watched as all the colours and energy that had been put into the lady's spirit body slowly descend like a rainbow waterfall into her physical body. When the colour had stopped ascending into the physical body, Henry gently lowered the spirit body back into the lady's physical body.

When the spirit body was back in the lady's physical body,

Henry proceeded to lift his hands off the side of the lady's head, and slowly disappeared back into the vibration of the room.

Within a few minutes, the vibration was back to that of the physical world.

My friend came to a few minutes later and explained that what she had experienced was like no healing she had ever had before. She felt herself floating, was aware of colours around her and felt completely at peace as if she had been surrounded with pure love. Needless to say, she had a good night's sleep after that healing!

Another friend who had an online healing was suffering from slight depression and lots of stress in his life. The gentleman decided to lie upon his bed, and I asked him to take in three deep breaths and then to relax within the motion of his breathing.

A few minutes had passed when I felt the coldness starting to swirl around my legs. I could feel the connection being made within the vibration between the spirit world, me and the gentleman's energy.

I watched as the vibration in the gentleman's room pixelated. I felt that I had become part of the energy. It was as if I was in the room with the gentleman. I then became aware of colour that was appearing. There were sparks of light and wisps of mist that were travelling all around the room.

I became aware of Henry standing behind the head of the gentleman as he lay on his bed. Henry moved closer and put his hands onto the top of the gentleman's head.

A green energy started to emanate through Henry's hands and connect into the gentleman's physical head. I observed as the green energy travelled down the full length of the physical body and then, after a few minutes, the spiritual body started to float out of the physical body and settle about a foot above the physical body.

Then there were two other spirit healers who appeared

and positioned themselves at either side of the gentleman's spiritual body, and they raised their hands above it. There was blue energy that appeared to be coming from their hands and entering into the spiritual body.

The blue energy was moving about and becoming part of the vibration inside the spiritual body. The blue energy was quite dark in colour and it started to grow in size. It was no longer just inside the spiritual body; it was now outside and appeared to be surrounding the spiritual body about two feet in circumference.

I watched as the two spiritual healers appeared to move their hands in unison as if they were conducting the flow of energy. As they did this, the blue colour became lighter in tone as if they were removing or diluting the density of the energy within the vibration of the gentleman's spiritual body.

They continued to do this for approximately five minutes before they stepped back and disappeared into the vibration of the room. I then watched Henry's hands change from green to white, and then white energy travelled through the gentleman's spiritual body incorporating the green and blue healing colours and changing them to white.

Henry then lowered the gentleman's spirit body back into his physical body before he disappeared into the vibration of the room. When the vibration had changed back from the spiritual to the physical, I then asked the gentleman to gently come back.

My friend explained that he had felt immense coldness around him. He had become aware of the colours before I had confirmed that I had seen them. He was feeling that an immense pressure had been lifted off his shoulders. He felt different, lighter.

Another friend had been complaining about back pain. He had been suffering with a stomach condition and severe back pain for quite some time but, like many people, he had learnt to suffer in silence and to live with the pain.

I asked my friend to lie upon his bed in his room and I watched as the vibration changed. I felt my energy connect with his energy, and became aware of quite a lot of spirit people who were present within the vibration in his room and in my office, where I was.

Once again, I had become aware of Henry who stepped forward and connected his hands onto each side of my friend's physical head, and an orange energy emanated from his hands covering the whole physical body. Henry then lifted my friend's spiritual body out of his physical body and held it in a controlled position about a foot above.

I watched as a spirit gentleman stepped forward and positioned himself on my friend's right-hand side around about his stomach area. The spirit healer then raised his hands above the spirit body, and yellow energy started to come out of his hands and into the stomach of the spirit body.

The yellow energy filled up the area across my friend's stomach, and then I was shown a picture of what I believe was his stomach and his intestines. The stomach and intestines were glowing in this yellow colour.

I observed with great interest as a tray of spiritual instruments appeared alongside him, and then the spirit surgeon picked up what appeared to be a spiritual one of these instruments and made an incision into the spirit body.

What I was watching intrigued me; the spirit surgeon appeared to be cutting away certain parts of the stomach and sewing back other parts. He proceeded to take the intestines and run his fingers along the outside of them as if he was checking them for blockages.

Another spirit surgeon arrived and stood next to the left-hand side of my friend's spirit body. The surgeon raised his hands over it, and this time red energy emanated from his hands and entered the spirit body.

I saw both surgeons working on my friend's spiritual body

under the control of Henry. The second surgeon, who was emanating the red energy, appeared to reach into the spiritual body and lift the spinal cord out.

I watched in amazement as this surgeon checked along the vertebrae in the spinal cord. The surgeon seemed to stop every so often and put what appeared to be a compound of some sort in between the vertebrae with a long thin instrument. He then used another strange instrument that was shaped like a hairdryer that he would place over the area of the vertebrae that the compound had been put into.

When this surgeon was finished, he placed the spinal cord back into my friend's spiritual body and he watched the other spiritual surgeon continue his work with great interest.

When the other spirit surgeon was finished, they both disappeared back into the vibration of the room and, once again, Henry's hands appeared to emanate white light that travelled all through my friend's spiritual body.

Henry lowered my friend's spiritual body back into his physical body and, after a few minutes, Henry disappeared into the vibration along with all the other spirit people who I was aware of in both rooms. I then asked my friend to come back to full consciousness.

My friend commented that he could not really explain what he had experienced. He said that he had felt as if his internal organs had been moving around inside him, and he was also experiencing the strangest of sensations like being touched although there was no-one in his room.

It was roughly about six months of experimenting with my guides with online healing before I offered this service on behalf of the spirit world to the public. This is the way they have developed it with me and I still find what I am shown fascinating and captivating every time an online healing takes place today.

Elementals In Healing

Elementals being involved in healing is something I had not really given a lot of thought to until I experienced some strange events while healing. I suppose there is no reason why they should not be involved as we are opening up to the vibration of the universal energy.

My First Elemental Experiences

The first time I became aware of the elemental world was when I was sitting at an open circle in the early stages of my development. I observed a little green fairy sitting on the edge of the table in the room. Another time, when I was lucky enough to see an elemental, was when a tree spirit entered our séance room in my home and was witnessed by a few members of the trance group. I have covered these early experiences in my previous book.

The first time I became aware of elementals involved in healing was when I had finished working with a lady at one of my healing clinics. I had just stepped back from the side of the healing bed and felt the energy of the guide slightly step back but not completely from me.

I was in a semi-conscious state of blending and was looking at the lady lying upon the bed when, all of a sudden, something caught my eye. I focused my vision onto the area that I had been drawn to and there, sitting on the lady's tummy, was a little green fairy! There was another standing on the end of the bed next to the lady's head and another standing on the lady's legs.

I looked on with disbelief but they were there! I could see them! I watched them for a few minutes, and then I felt the energy around me start to change and I was no longer blending with the guide. I looked again at the lady but this time the fairies had disappeared.

I had a friend who is a spiritual medium who was sitting in as an observer that day. She had seen me staring at the lady for about five minutes and, when the client had left the room, she said to me, "Did you see something strange with the lady?" I admitted to her that I had but, before I could tell her about my experience, my friend asked, "Did you see fairies?" "I did see them," I revealed.

She went on to say that they had appeared about ten minutes into the healing and they had constantly moved around the bed. They were walking, standing and sitting upon the client all through the healing. She said it was fascinating to watch, and she could barely believe her eyes when they had appeared.

This was a wonderful experience to have been shown and be part of but, what made it even more special for me, was that it was shared with a medium friend which was additional confirmation of the reality of the elemental world.

Floating Guide

Another strange experience or phenomenon that takes place with my healing practice is being aware of a healing guide that may not be from the vibration of the spirit world. I will let you decide for yourself.

This strange sensation first happened with working with a little boy who has cystic fibrosis. The little boy's grandmother was present. She is a working spiritual medium, and the observer with me that day was my friend who is another spiritual medium. The two ladies have known each other for many years.

The little boy was less than a year old. I gently laid him upon the healing bed and I went into the blending process with one of my guides. This guide checked everything was good to go, and then the blending of the energy changed and another healing guide blended into my energy.

It was roughly about ten minutes into the healing when the

energy of the blending started to change again. This time the energy felt completely different; it is hard to explain but it felt as if I was the guide. I was floating in and out of the energy of this guide's vibration, as if I were inside the guide's vibration and I had become one with the guide.

I looked down and saw the little boy. He was about three feet below me lying on the bed. I could see myself holding my right hand on to his head and my left hand on his chest. I observed the energy of the guide working through me and it appeared black in colour. It did not have arms or fingers like a human. What I could see was long strands of energy that looked like fingers that were about two feet in length.

The vibration of the guide seemed to float up and down, above and over the little boy and my physical body that was fixed around the bed. The guide put his long-looking fingers over the chest of the little boy and moved them backwards and forwards as if scanning over the lungs and chest area. Then the movement of the guide's fingers stopped and the black energy appeared to enter the area of the lungs of the little boy. This transfer of energy took place for a short while and I then felt the vibration of the blending start to retract. After a short period, I was aware that I was back in my physical body.

I looked at the little boy lying on the bed; he was fast asleep. I glanced over in the direction of the grandmother and the observer. The grandmother was just staring at the healing bed.

After a few minutes had passed, she came over to her grandson, picked him up from the healing bed and cradled him in her arms.

The grandmother explained that she did not know what was working through me during the healing. She said that the energy had no legs, and floated up and down at the side of the bed. It had long creepy-looking fingers and was completely black in colour.

The other medium, who was the observer that day, was

trying to explain to the grandmother that, as she was a working medium, she should understand that sometimes those who work through us may not be from the vibration of the spirit world. The medium went on to say that she had seen this healing guide working with me on a number of occasions and, for her, it was wonderful to be able talk openly about it with a fellow medium as they both watched the healing take place.

This guide still works through me from time to time and, although I do not know if this guide is part of the spirit world or from another dimension, I do know that this unusual guide has to come through my doorkeeper to work with me. This means that this guide is a trusted part of my healing team who assemble around me.

Angels Within Healing

I have had the vision of angels while healing a few times over the years. The first experience I had was when my life was in a little turmoil with my own emotions. I had been pondering for a while if the path of mediumship was really my calling.

I remember sitting in a grassy meadow meditating with a development group when, all of a sudden, I was looking at a bright white light that appeared in the distance. I watched intently as the bright light drew closer and closer to me. The white light stopped in front of me and I saw a pair of white wings appear from the light. I watched as the white wings hovered within the white light. Then I saw what I can only describe as the image of an angel.

The angel descended from the white light and, within seconds, was standing alongside me. The angel opened out his wings and a white light engulfed him. He then got down onto his knees and wrapped his beautiful white wings around me. I was, at that very moment, overtaken with feelings of love and protection, peace and tranquillity.

The angel stayed with his wings wrapped around me for about five minutes before standing up. He then opened his wings and, with the easiest of a flutter, he rose back up into the white light and disappeared.

I did not understand what this encounter with the angel signified, but I had the strangest feeling afterwards that the path I would choose to follow would involve the spirit world.

Another Encounter With An Angel

I had been working with a young girl who had a brain tumour and, throughout the healing taking place, I was experiencing an overwhelming sensation of love within the blending with my guide. I could see the healing energy that appeared to be wrapped around the young girl.

The healing energy was moving under the direction of my hands controlled by the guide. I was mesmerised at how the energy was reacting to every movement. When the guide stopped my hands from moving, the energy appeared to stop moving, and if the guide moved his hands in another direction, the energy followed.

When the healing had concluded, I felt the blending with the guide starting to retract and I found myself standing at the end of the bed where the young girl's head was lying. I looked down to the bottom of the bed and saw a vision of an angel. This was completely different from the first time I had seen an angel; this one could not be more dissimilar in appearance.

I was looking at an image of a shape similar to what you would find representing an angel decoration on a Christmas tree. This image was glowing white in colour as if it was pulsating, and it was just floating at the bottom of the bed. I watched with great interest for a good few minutes before the image disappeared, and I felt myself become completely separated from the blending with my guide.

Another time I experienced an angel was again at a healing clinic. I was working with a gentleman who had arrived with a concern regarding a problem with his liver. I had just sat down to begin the blending process when my attention was drawn to the bottom of the bed.

I saw a little spirit light that appeared to sparkle like glitter. The spirit light started to become longer and the light become stronger. The light stretched and grew in size until it appeared to look about six feet in height and just floated in mid-air. Then the light became brighter and brighter.

I was not alarmed at what I was witnessing. I was in awe of the presence of this spiritual being who had come forward to show itself. There was an overwhelming feeling of love that emanated from this being. The energy had a calming influence which appeared to connect with me. The white light started to diminish after about five minutes and I then returned to the process of blending with the healing guide.

Angels or higher beings appear to carry an energy that emanates love through their vibration. In my experiences with them, they have always emanated a glowing white light around themselves and brought an understanding that everything will be OK.

Spirit Inventions

A gentleman got in touch to ask if I would send distant healing to a member of his family. The family member was a child who was less than a year old. The child had a problem with his heart and was in Great Ormond Street Hospital.

That evening I sat with the intention of sending distant healing through the connection with a healing guide from The Healing Ministry from the spirit side of life. I felt the energy of the guide come forward and quickly realised it was Henry. Henry asked if I would like to travel with him to visit the child in hospital. "Of course," was my reply.

All of a sudden, I found myself travelling through a grey-looking mist for a few minutes. I arrived at a hospital building, went through the doors, upstairs and into a room where the little child was lying upon a bed. The infant had tubes and wires attached to him and there were lots of machines that were all around him. I was standing alongside Henry but he was not the only spirit worker present within the room.

The room was busy with spirit healers, doctors, surgeons and a couple of nurses, and that was not counting the medical team who were working with the child in the physical world. I looked around the room and saw the strangest thing. There was a machine that looked like a transparent box with metal surrounding it above the bed of the little boy.

The box had what looked like a spiritual heart that was inside it. There were clear tubes that were attached into both sides of the box and what appeared to be blood being pumped into one side of the heart and out the other side. The tubes that were attached to the box appeared to be connected to the child who was lying upon the bed.

I watched as the spiritual heart was beating inside this spiritual box above the bed of the infant boy. I asked Henry,

"What is this above the bed?" He replied that it was a medical invention that had been developed on their side of life that had not been invented in the physical world yet. I was prompted to join in with Henry and the other healers within the room to sending healing energy into the spirit of the little boy.

A short period of time had passed when I felt my energy starting to travel back to my room in my house. When I arrived home, I sat and thought about what had taken place during the healing, and what I had seen with this new type of invention from the spirit world that was keeping the little child's spirit heart alive. The little boy pulled through after being in hospital and is living a healthy life.

A few months later, I was watching television and a programme came on about a new medical invention that had been developed that could keep a liver functioning with a blood supply without having to go through the old procedure of putting it on ice before a transplant. I then realised what I had seen in the room above the bed of the little child in hospital, and it all started to make sense.

Spirit Teaching Me To Understand Healing

I suppose no-one really understands their mediumistic journey at the beginning. Saying that, I have always been blown away with what I have experienced and been shown by the spirit world.

When I started my journey into the world of trance healing, it was all about learning to get the connection right with my guides through the attunement process. When the healing with a client got underway, I would see the healing energy in waves of colour around the person receiving the healing. The energy would flow in a controlled manner in the direction of the movement made by my hands under the influence of the guide. This experience with waves of energy still fascinates me today.

I would constantly experiment with the flow of energy or

vibration coming through my hands and fingers. I would ask the observer who was present during a healing to put their hands between my hands and the client, and feel the vibration as it hit onto their hands. Then I would ask the spirit world to allow the energy to pass through the observer's hand into the client without the observer feeling the energy vibration.

Usually, the person who is between the healer and the client would not feel any energy because the healing energy is not for the observer but, when asked for the spirit world to show the vibration, they never failed.

I would move my fingers vigorously about three feet above the client's body creating a trickle of energy to see what they could feel. The clients said that they felt as if they were being sprinkled with water. I would ask the spirit world to heat up the energy coming through my hands, and then ask them to make it colder. The spirit world would make one of my hands roasting and the other ice cold when practising and experimenting with healing.

The spirit world started to show me organs that were orange in colour in the physical body of the people who were getting the healing. They would use Latin words which meant nothing to me as I did not understand what they meant. Then they started to use words that made sense to me e.g. liver, kidney etc.

They started to lift spirit organs out of the physical bodies of the clients and would work on them directly and, when they were finished, they would lower them back into the client's physical body.

I remember, on one occasion, when a client came with a blood disorder and I became part of a blood cell and travelled inside the bloodstream of the client. I kept thinking about the film Innerspace! This was an experience that I will never forget.

I would feel the trance healing vibration travel through the body of the clients in waves of energy connecting into certain organs within the spirit body. The spirit world would connect onto parts of the client's anatomy, and my hands would become fixed upon that spot and I would not be able to move them. Believe me, I tried on numerous occasions.

I sat regularly, blending with my guides for development, and the healing energy got more intense. I would close my eyes while doing a trance healing, and an hour and a half would pass and it would feel as if I had just closed my eyes. The spirit world had control of me through the blending process and then the psychic surgery made an appearance.

When the psychic surgery was proposed by the spirit world, I truly thought I had lost the plot but, instead of interfering with what was taking place, I just ran with it. I suppose, by then, I completely trusted my guides to have control over me when they blended for healing.

The journey of discovery into the workings of psychic surgery truly opened my eyes to the possibilities of healing, and what could and has been achieved through trusting those who work with us from the spirit side of life.

I can recall when a lady came to one of the clinics with a brain tumour. I watched as the spirit surgeon slowly drilled into the lady's spiritual head by turning a winder on an instrument that looked like it was from the Victorian era. The surgeon gently removed a circular piece of bone that had been cut out with the circular drill and then he proceeded to use instruments directly on the lady's spiritual brain. He removed what appeared to be a grey mass then replaced the circular bone back into the hole in the skull.

I have watched spirit surgeons completely strip down spiritual kneecaps and rebuild them. In addition, they have worked with people with spinal conditions when the spiritual spine has been completely lifted out of the physical body and the surgeon has put a type of compound in between the vertebrae and, on other occasions, they have put brackets secured with screws along the spinal cord.

I have watched operations taking place where the spirit stomach has been completely opened up and the intestines have been laid out in front of me, allowing the spirit surgeons to operate on them before carefully replacing them back into the spiritual body of the client.

They have worked on clients' eyes, noses, ears, throats, bladders, kidneys, hearts, pancreas, lungs and lots and lots of other medical conditions that clients have come seeking help with over the years.

The knowledge and guidance that they have shared with me over many years regarding healing and mediumship has been a huge learning curve in my life. I now truly understand that all spiritual healing energy is contained within the vibrational energy that they bring when they attune their vibration into our vibration. We, as healers, are only the vessel or channel for the healing energy to pass through to the spirit of the client.

It is important to remember that we, as healers, cannot cure any ailment or condition within the mind, spirit or physical body of a client on our own. The vibrational healing energy that they bring to us belongs to the divine source and, when we trust those who work with us from the spirit side of life, the possibilities of what can be achieved are endless.

All these wonderful experiences of trance healing and psychic surgery over the years have taught me to trust unconditionally, and to develop a strong working relationship with those wise beings in the spirit world. I used to question everything during the early stages of my healing journey but I never question spirit anymore. I just give myself over to them when they come forward to work through me without question.

The more you trust your guides and your spirit team then the greater the flow of healing energy which will pass through you, enabling them to have more freedom to bring forward greater results from the healing energy.

The spirit world is constantly bringing new ways of doing

things with us within our mediumship. My understanding and knowledge of healing is constantly evolving. The way I conduct a healing today is not the same as I would have conducted it six months ago. The reason for this is that my chemical composition and understanding of the healing vibration is constantly changing with my development.

It is important to remember that if you are working as a healer and your spiritual progression is not evolving then there is something not quite right within your mediumistic development.

The spirit world is about advancement on your spiritual journey. The more you allow them to sit and blend with you, the more they are able to bring you through time. This will help your understanding and knowledge through the vibrational energy.

The spirit world is never idle. They are constantly working away at developing new ways of doing things to help humanity.

I mentioned earlier about the new energy that is being developed by the spirit world that was safer for physical mediums within a séance. They are calling it, to my understanding, "**light** force energy" and now I would like to explain about my experiences with the new type of energy that is being developed within the world of healing that is being called "**life** force energy". The slightly different names denote the purpose for the use of the energy within the different realms of mediumship.

Life Force Healing

I have been guided by Henry all throughout my development. His words have always been an inspiration to me and I have always followed his lead without question.

This type of healing energy has been developed on the spirit side of life, although I have been experimenting with it with my guides for a while and it truly is a unique way for them to use this vibrational energy within healing. I do not fully understand it at this moment in time but I hope to be able to teach it in the future when I do.

The first time I experienced this type of healing was when I was experimenting with my friend a few years ago. This was the healing I mentioned earlier when the energy connected onto her spiritual bladder and, after giving it a little squeeze, my friend had to run to the toilet!

The wonderful thing about the experiment back then, and something that always fascinates me about the spirit world, is that they are always taking the opportunity to experiment with us for development for the future without us realising.

I was speaking with a client who had arrived at one of the clinics with a cancerous condition. The prognosis from the hospital was not what the client had hoped for at his consultation.

I explained to the client that I could not guarantee anything apart from the understanding that the spirit world would come forward when asked, to see what they could do to help with his condition. I also went on to explain that he was under the guidance of his consultant at the hospital at all times and that all alternative therapies were complementary.

I asked the gentleman to lie upon the healing bed. I had gone into an altered state when I heard Henry's voice saying that they were going to experiment with a new way of working with energy, and I was to listen to what was being said and follow their direction.

I felt the blending taking place and could sense that the energy that was connecting with me felt different. This energy was alive and I had the strangest of sensations within the blending that I had become one with the vibration in the room.

I found myself standing alongside the middle of the healing bed, where the gentleman's stomach was. Henry asked me to put my hands over the top of the gentleman's stomach about a foot in height above. He then said, "I want you to feel into the vibration that is around you. Do not think about it but just relax and allow yourself to become one with the vibration." He repeated these instructions constantly as I let myself go into this new vibration.

Henry asked, "Do you feel the vibrational energy?" "Yes, I do." "Now allow the energy to become one through your hands and into the client." I could feel vibrations coming through my hands and connecting into the cancerous mass within the gentleman's stomach area. The vibrational energy became fixated upon that area. I could not move my hands away from it.

Henry then said, "Now, do you feel the vibration becoming part of the cancerous growth?" "Yes, I can feel it." "Explain to me what you feel," he urged. "I can feel the energy attached to the mass. It feels like I am becoming part of the composition of it. It feels like I am the cancerous mass." "Well done, that's what we are looking for from you."

"What is this I'm experiencing?" I asked him. "This is a new type of vibrational healing energy that we have been developing on our side of life for some time. It is in the early stages of development and we are learning about how to connect it into the vibration of life on your side. Now what else do you feel?" "I can feel the structure of the mass and I feel as if the vibration of the energy wants to break down the chemical composition of the cancerous mass. It feels as if the energy wants to change the structure." "Excellent!" he declared. "Now gently start to feel the vibration releasing its grip from the cancer."

I could feel the vibration releasing its hold from the cancerous mass and the energy in the room start to change back into the trance blending energy. I continued to proceed with the trance healing with the gentleman who was lying upon the bed.

Henry went on to mention that this new type of healing would be brought into the physical world at some time in the future but there was lots of development to be done on their side and on our side. "What do I call it?" I asked him. "It will be known as 'life force healing'."

After a short time, I finished the healing session with the gentleman. This experience has opened up a new chapter within my development in the world of healing, and I have been experimenting with it regularly under the guidance of Henry.

A lady came for healing who had been involved in the world of spirit for quite some time, and I asked her if it would be OK to allow the spirit world to experiment with her with this new type of healing. The lady agreed and lay upon the healing bed. I asked her to close her eyes and to talk openly about any sensation or feelings that she may experience while the healing took place.

This time I closed my eyes and gently started to breathe into the vibration within the room and, after a few minutes, I was connected into the vibration of life. I was aware of Henry standing alongside me.

I had discussed with the lady before the healing about what was causing her concern, and she explained that she was having some issues with her ovaries and her stomach area. I proceeded to go down to the general area of the lady's pelvis and, once again under the direction of Henry's guidance, I felt the vibrational energy connect into the lady's right ovary. I could feel the energy which was coming through my hands become one with the ovary.

Under the guidance of Henry, I was directed to move my hands upwards and downwards above the area of the ovary. I did this motion for a few minutes before moving my hands across to the other ovary and repeating the same procedure.

I then moved my hands above the stomach area of the lady and, once again, the energy locked at a certain position and I could not move it. The vibrational energy appears to become one with vibration of the client, and feels like it is restructuring the chemical composition within the area that is causing the client concern.

I then moved my hands above the chest area of the lady and felt the energy connect into her heart area. After some time had passed, Henry then asked for me to start to feel the energy release from the vibration of the lady and to gently bring myself back.

The lady has kindly offered to put in her own words what she felt during the healing and what she experienced after that day so you can hear it directly from her.

I first heard about Chris and his healing work around three years ago as one of my family members had visited his clinic and had a healing on her hip (she was in constant pain and discomfort due to arthritis). She commented on how much better and easier it felt to move after his healing session.

I was going through a hard emotional time around this point in my life. I thought I'd give Chris a phone and arrange an appointment as I wanted to try a more natural way of helping me with my situation, rather than just relying on a doctor and medication.

On the day, I nervously entered the clinic. I wasn't sure what to expect but Chris made me feel relaxed right away with his calm voice and relaxed demeanour. He explained how the healing procedure worked and I told him about how I was feeling ill due to anxiety, lack of sleep and what was causing these issues that I really needed healing for.

I lay down upon the healing bed, closed my eyes and started to relax to the beautiful Gregorian chant music that filled the room, and Chris got to work on the healing. Straight away, I felt the temperature in the room get colder. It felt like I was surrounded in a cocoon of peace and tranquillity. It was so relaxing and almost like I was drifting away, like floating in a pool of water. It really was such a beautiful relaxing feeling.

I felt like the treatment room we were in was full of people and, even though my eyes were closed the whole time, I felt a deep, warm energy flow from my head down to my feet. I saw so many colours: purples, greens, yellows, and it felt wonderful! As Chris's healing energy started to withdraw, all the pent-up emotions that I had seemed to release, leading me to cry uncontrollably. It felt like a plug had been pulled from me and everything that I had been harbouring within me for a long time was now coming away.

After a few minutes had passed, I then started to laugh. I felt embarrassed at what was happening with me and my emotions, but Chris softly explained that this was normal and just to let it all release from me. When the healing was finished, I felt exhausted and relaxed at the same time and so much better within myself as if a weight had been lifted from me.

The next day, I didn't feel ill or anxious like I had been for a long time and I also slept like a baby. It was the best night's sleep that I had in months. This was the start of many healings that I have had with Chris and his spirit team over the last few years.

In one of my recent healing sessions, Chris asked if he could try "life force healing". He explained that it was a new form of healing that his spirit team had been experimenting with, and he would like me to experience it. I was excited about this as it was new to me and I wanted to give it a try.

I lay down once again upon the healing bed, got myself comfortable and closed my eyes. Within a few minutes, I could feel my right ovary being moved about. It wasn't a sore experience, in fact it felt strangely relaxing. With my eyes still closed, Chris asked me to try to explain to him what I was feeling.

I explained to him in detail all the sensations and feelings that I was experiencing, and then he asked me to open my eyes. As I did this, I quickly focused onto the area that I had been feeling where the sensations had been taking place within my body.

I could see whips of what looked like white string-looking energy coming from his fingertips above my hip, pointing down over my ovary. He'd been doing exactly what I had felt and I couldn't believe the white, string-like energy coming from his fingertips! He did this again on another part of my body. With my eyes closed, he asked me to tell him when I felt any sensations again. Within a minute or so, I could feel my heart gently vibrating or being slightly tugged.

I opened my eyes and saw that Chris had his hand above me, pointing down towards my heart and I saw the white, string-like energy coming from his fingertips again. I was absolutely amazed at what I felt and saw, and also the fact that he could manipulate parts of the inner body without touching them!

After I experienced Chris's life force healing, we agreed that he would use the technique on my stomach problems as I occasionally get IBS and cramps. So again, lying down completely relaxed and excited to see how this would help my stomach issues, Chris started the healing.

Straight away I felt coldness on one part of my stomach and heat on the other side. I felt movement and a few tugs within my stomach area. I continued to feel completely relaxed. I felt spirit standing to the left-hand side of me and cold breezes sweep over my legs. It was quite a powerful experience and I look forward to more healing like this. My stomach felt so much lighter and the bloating and cramps I'd been experiencing earlier had disappeared.

I think this is a good opportunity to allow other clients to explain what they have felt and experienced in their own words before, during and after receiving a healing.

Healing Testimonials

I first met Chris around two and a half years ago, as he was recommended to me through a friend. At that time, I had been suffering for many years with a really painful condition in my neck and back due to an old injury from 20 years previously. It would start off as an ache in my neck and back which would increase painfully over the days to horrendous spasms, which would last for a few days before the pain would subside but only to restart all over again a few weeks later. I had been back and forth over the years to my GP who started prescribing me medication, which just dulled the pain and made me feel woozy.

In due course, I had referrals to numerous physiotherapists, all to no avail. I met Chris around the time of a very bad flare-up. He was a very friendly man who listened to me intently. He said that he couldn't promise to cure me but, hopefully, he could alleviate some of my pain. I was then asked to lie down on his healing bed, close my eyes and relax while soft chanting music played in the background.

As I relaxed, I started to become aware of the colour purple coming in bursts in my mind's eye, swirling and swaying from side to side. I then became aware of the feeling that my body was rising from his couch, although I was still lying there. I felt like I had risen a few inches and still don't really know how to explain that to this day.

After a few moments, I became aware of a presence in the room, which to me was impossible as there was only myself, Chris and an observer sitting in the corner. I can only describe what I felt next as like small feathery movements in my neck and back followed by very light tugging movements.

It was around this point that I saw a man's face in my head. He looked to be in his 30s with dark curly hair and light-tanned skin. He gave me a reassuring smile as if to say, "I am here to help and I am going to make you better." The healing session ended soon after and I explained to Chris what I had felt and seen. He then gave me instruction on my after care and explained that healing would still be taking place on me well after I had left.

Ten minutes after I left, I got extremely fatigued and could smell what I can only describe as an anaesthetic smell on myself. I felt exactly the same as I had a few years before when waking up after an operation. My pain level was so much better when I left Chris that day and, by day four, the pain was completely gone.

Since attending healing with Chris and his spirit team, I have felt transformed. I feel that my healings have been journeys rather than procedures. As Chris and his team begin to work, I feel as though I am under a form of anaesthetic, seeing waves of blue and green light and shadow while being aware of spirit presence, repetition of sounds and messages often come around. I once experienced spirit giving me guidance and an illustration of a choice I was afraid to make.

There is always a unique calmness while spirit is working. My body feels that it is somewhere tranquil and special. All my stress dissipates and I can easily let go of emotion and anxiety. It can take some time to come round from the healing session; there is always a reluctance to leave the comfort of being "there".

I have felt light anaesthesia for some days after a session. On one occasion, I felt an instrument entering my partial problematic right ovary. There was no pain, just pressure and a freeing sensation around the area. Over the next few nights, I would wake up feeling the sensation repeatedly. My ovarian pain was less and I believe cysts were removed. Working on my pubis symphysis and pelvis has meant that I seldom have the chronic hip and coccyx pain that I have suffered with for 22 years.

My falls have lessened as I have less numbness and more balance with my gait. Ovarian and internal gynaecological problems have almost disappeared. My overall health and mobility have improved dramatically. I will continue to have Chris and his wonderful team work with me.

I began attending Chris's clinic shortly after my dad passed away. Until this point, I had only associated healing with physical ailments. I was apprehensive on my first visit but Chris was great and very reassuring.

The work Chris does really needs to be felt to truly understand and appreciate it. It's mind-blowing! You lie on the healing bed, eyes closed, begin to relax and go deeper and deeper, but you are still aware of the surroundings. I love this feeling. I always experience a personal light show, usually warm whites and deep purples that fade, leaving behind shapes and outlines, some I recognise, some I do not.

Many times, I have needed to release emotions that are too painful. Most of the time I am unaware that this is what I need to do! But Chris switches the tap, and I cry. A proper gut-wrenching, body-rocking cry, that I have absolutely no control over, no matter how hard I try! Then, in the blink of an eye, a new warm loving energy of total comfort, a spreading bright light flowing through my head and I instantly feel that my balance has been restored. I know that it is thanks to Chris and his spirit team that I have managed to stay off medication that numbs me. Chris has made the most awful heartbreaking time bearable.

I first visited Chris for healing to see if he could help me with anger and emotional issues I had been suffering from childhood. I had tried everything to help deal with the issue but nothing had worked.

As soon as the healing started, I felt a lovely warm feeling of energy through my whole body. It got stronger around my stomach area to the point I could feel all the anger and emotions in the pit of my stomach rising up through my body to my throat where I felt an urge to get all the negative energy out my body through my mouth. It felt like my heart had been opened a little and everything that I had stored for the past 30 years was being released. I had an uncontrollable urge to just cry and get rid of everything.

Towards the end of the healing session, I felt the spirit team finishing their work and closing everything down and felt calmness again. It was a very powerful and positive experience for me, and one I will never forget. For the first time in my life, the past no longer makes me angry or hurt. The past doesn't matter to me anymore.

Chris and his spirit team have helped me in a big way and I can't thank them enough for the work they have done.

I had visited numerous doctors and therapists regarding my stomach condition. The results were always the same. It would feel good for a short period, then back to square one. I was travelling in Scotland and, through a friend, I heard about a healer called Chris Ratter. From what I had read and heard about him, I was very curious about his work and, of course, if it could help me. I am a spiritual medium myself and have seen many miracles that the spirit world has done.

Through one of my friends, I managed to get an appointment with Chris, and I had an excited and positive feeling within me. When I arrived, it was a warm welcoming atmosphere, and Chris explained the process, about how it works. His wife was in the room as an observer, which gave a nice impression as this was something new to me.

I was asked to lie down on a healing bed, Chris was talking and I could clearly feel the spirit energy immediately. It didn't take long before I felt like I was asleep (I think that's the best way of explaining).

I opened my eyes about 30 minutes later, had a glass of

water and a comforting talk with Chris, just to make sure that everything was OK with me.

I got some feedback on what had happened and where Chris and his spirit team had worked. I asked Gail what she had seen and she explained that they had been working in the area of my stomach. I had felt that someone was working inside my stomach, moving things around as if I were having my inner stomach operated upon. The strange feeling continued in my stomach and it lasted through the next day. I have not had any problem with my stomach since then.

The healing I received that day was totally different from any other healing that I have ever experienced before. I have visited Chris a few times since that day and every time is a new experience.

I met Chris in August 2018 at a demonstration he did for charity at a Spiritualist church near where I live. I was spellbound by his story and, having been involved in trance mediumship myself for many years, spoke to him afterwards about it. I went home and sent him a friend request on social media. To be honest, I think a part of me knew that I would be requiring his services in the future.

Another "chance" meeting took place a month later in September 2018 when I attended another charity event. This one was hosted by my best friend's dad and I spent a long time talking to my friend's sister-in-law. This conversation eventually led me to read extensively on the effect of food on human health. During this research, I also learnt about the potentially devastating effects of mainstream cancer treatment on the body.

The moment that these two events were preparing me for arrived in the summer of 2020 when I was diagnosed with breast cancer. I knew it was cancer from the moment I researched the difference between a benign cyst and malignant tumour. My blood ran cold as I read a description of skin "puckering" around a cancerous tumour and I knew in that moment what I was facing. I also asked my guides who confirmed it was cancer. When the nurse from the hospital rang to deliver the official diagnosis following a biopsy, she was quite taken aback by my calm response. The truth was, after confirmation through my own intuition and asking my guides directly, I would have been more surprised if she was phoning to say I was in the clear!

I knew from my research that I did not want to go down the traditional route of cancer treatment, so I rejected all hospital appointments opting instead for spiritual healing and altering my diet again. As regards diet, I was already three-quarters of the way there after my second "chance" meeting which was completely orchestrated by those wiser, loving souls in the world of spirit.

I asked my guides if seeing Chris was something I should pursue. The answer was a strong "yes". This was backed up by the fact that Chris was able to fit me in weekly and ran his Edinburgh clinic on my day off. Everything came together perfectly so I knew, beyond doubt, that healing with Chris and his spirit team was right for me.

My first session with Chris was remarkable to say the least. We chatted beforehand, and he made it clear that although miracles weren't guaranteed, they can and do happen. As he worked with his spirit team, I could feel my tumour go numb. It was clear to me that there was a lot going on and that they were all working hard to help me.

When the healing was over, I reluctantly came back to full consciousness and felt quite emotional. The love and gentle compassion from those in spirit was palpable, and I felt blessed to be in a position to know about and be able to access such magic.

I saw Chris every week from August 2020 right through to the next national coronavirus lockdown. Every single week the healing was different. Sometimes I felt extremely cold, sometimes warm and sometimes both! Chris explained that this was due to the different types of healing energy that his spirit team was using.

One week it felt like I was lying on an electric blanket but everything else was freezing cold. It was as if those in spirit were doing their best to keep me comfortable which was really touching. The interesting thing was that the electric blanket feeling started before Chris commenced the healing, so I can completely relate to his description of his spirit team preparing everything in advance for the good of the patient.

One week that definitely stands out in my mind is the time I witnessed Chuckles popping in.

I have had mediumistic experiences my whole life and, although I'm not currently working as a medium, I have done a bit in the past but not in recent years. This is why I wasn't expecting to see anything clairvoyantly or hear anything clairaudiently. On this occasion, I saw in my mind's eye someone looking over me with their head close to mine. The image was so strong that I actually opened my eyes to see if Chris was peering at me. I could see his arm above me so I knew that this had been a spirit person. I also heard the name "John" called in.

Afterwards, I told Chris what I had seen and heard. He asked me to describe the person I saw. I said, "He wasn't an adult and he wasn't a child but he wasn't a teenager either, if that makes sense." To my astonishment, Chris said it did. He said Chuckles had made an appearance.

He usually shows himself as a child but he is actually an old soul which is why I couldn't pinpoint an age for him.

As regards John, I asked if Chris could understand the name and he said he had an uncle in spirit with this name. I had been reading Chris's first book Mediumship Within and, when I got home, I continued where I had left off. The first paragraph I read on my return regarded Chris's uncle who he didn't name in the book. No prizes for guessing his name! This was confirmation for me that what I was experiencing both physically and mediumistically during healing was genuine.

Experiencing trance healing when you have done trance mediumship, I would guess is a bit different. I sometimes feel spirit blending with me as I lie on the healing bed. This is always welcome as I love feeling the different energies that the spirit people bring forward.

Another fascinating experience I had during healing with Chris and his spirit team was feeling spiritual anaesthesia. I often jerk with the amount of energy running through my spiritual and physical bodies. It seems to happen when the spirit team are "operating" on the tumour within my spiritual body. One week, I felt as if a heavy blanket was on top of me and I didn't want to move. It wasn't unpleasant but quite comforting. Chris told me afterwards that I had been given a spiritual anaesthetic to stop me from moving during a complex part of the operation. I was astounded but also felt privileged to have experienced such an amazing feeling.

Chris and his healing spirit team have and will play a crucial role in what I trust will be my recovery (although, at the time of writing, I am still in this process). I am certain there has been positive progression with my health since I started seeing Chris and following a strict diet. The puckering around the tumour is definitely less pronounced. I truly believe if I continue with my alternative healing route of which Chris and his healing spirit team play a huge role, I will eventually be cancer-free.

Perception Of The Spirit World

I suppose there is much deliberation on what the spirit world truly is. Many people have their own beliefs and ideas as to what it actually is but I like to think upon it as heaven, a place we step into after our transition from the physical world into the world of spirit. A place where we meet up with our loved ones and friends who have passed over before us, where there is perfect harmony and unconditional love for all. A place where all can continue to evolve and live for eternity.

We understand that when in the spirit world, we no longer need to carry the physical body after we have transcended back into heaven, and the reason for this is that the physical body is used purely as the overcoat that we wear in the material world when we are here.

If we are to believe this to be correct, then the true essence of who we are is the life force energy within our own physical body that we call our spirit and, when we transcend, then we connect it back into the vibration of the spirit world or heaven. Therefore, the world of spirit must be a collective life force energy that sustains all living energy within its own vibration.

I would like to believe that the spirit world may just be on a slightly different vibration to our world, parallel but in a different time zone to ours. The spirit world may be a few seconds or minutes ahead of our time and we would never know that their world was there alongside ours, just out of sight or reach from many until it is time for our spirit within to return home.

When we learn to raise our vibration through different means of development, e.g. sitting in the power, meditation etc., this allows us to tap in one way or another to the world of the unseen as it is often referred to in many circles or otherwise known as the world of spirit.

When we make reference to mediums learning to raise their vibration, what is really happening is they are learning to understand the vibration that surrounds us by allowing their own vibrational energy to connect into the vibration of life that is all around us all the time.

They are learning to become one with the vibration of life, allowing them to look beyond the veil between the two worlds and to connect into the vibration of the spirit world, when they have attuned themselves to the vibrational energy.

When I think about the elemental world and the work that they do, I often wonder where they come from and where their world is. I often think about the spirit world being on another vibration to our world and why not the elemental world as well. These strange thoughts started me thinking about the possibility that they are actually living in our world or close to it but just out of sight.

We understand from books that have been written and folklore that has been passed down through the generations by word of mouth that elementals are tending to mother earth's needs. This would lead us to believe that they are either in the vibration of our world for short periods or they are here all the time helping nature.

When the vibrational energy has been right, people have stated that they have been able to see them from time to time but only when they appear to allow it. I suppose they have to trust the people who they are showing themselves to. It makes complete sense to me that their world is the same idea as the world of spirit, where they live in a different vibration or a different timeline to ours.

We know that they must be in our world to be able to nourish the plant life, trees etc. and we know that their energy vibration has been used in healing and in séances, as I have mentioned earlier in the book. With this in mind, they must be coming to us through a different vibration and, the more we can learn to connect into the vibration around us, the closer all the vibrational worlds will become.

I suppose what I am talking about is quantum physics and, although our scientists are learning more about this subject, it will be interesting to see what we understand about it in the future.

Physical Mediumship

Physical mediumship is the ultimate proof of life after death and I am looking forward to covering this truly unique phenomenon. I have barely scratched the surface of what it is, and what it entails to develop and become a physical medium, but I think I will keep this for my next book!

**6TH
BOOKS**

ALL THINGS PARANORMAL

Investigations, explanations and deliberations on the paranormal,
supernatural, explainable or unexplainable. 6th Books seeks to
give answers while nourishing the soul: whether making use of the
scientific model or anecdotal and fun, but always
beautifully written.
Titles cover everything within parapsychology: how to, lifestyles,
alternative medicine, beliefs, myths and theories.
If you have enjoyed this book, why not tell other readers by
posting a review on your preferred book site?

Recent bestsellers from 6th Books are:

The Afterlife Unveiled
What the Dead Are Telling us About Their World!
Stafford Betty
What happens after we die? Spirits speaking through mediums
know, and they want us to know. This book unveils their world...
Paperback: 978-1-84694-496-3 ebook: 978-1-84694-926-5

Spirit Release
Sue Allen
A guide to psychic attack, curses, witchcraft, spirit attachment,
possession, soul retrieval, haunting, deliverance, exorcism and
more, as taught at the College of Psychic Studies.
Paperback: 978-1-84694-033-0 ebook: 978-1-84694-651-6

I'm Still With You
True Stories of Healing Grief Through Spirit Communication
Carole J. Obley
A series of after-death spirit communications which uplift, comfort
and heal, and show how love helps us grieve.
Paperback: 978-1-84694-107-8 ebook: 978-1-84694-639-4

Less Incomplete
A Guide to Experiencing the Human Condition Beyond the
Physical Body
Sandie Gustus
Based on 40 years of scientific research, this book is a dynamic
guide to understanding life beyond the physical body.
Paperback: 978-1-84694-351-5 ebook: 978-1-84694-892-3

Advanced Psychic Development
Becky Walsh
Learn how to practise as a professional, contemporary spiritual medium.
Paperback: 978-1-84694-062-0 ebook: 978-1-78099-941-8

Astral Projection Made Easy
and overcoming the fear of death
Stephanie June Sorrell
From the popular Made Easy series, *Astral Projection Made Easy* helps to eliminate the fear of death, through discussion of life beyond the physical body.
Paperback: 978-1-84694-611-0 ebook: 978-1-78099-225-9

The Miracle Workers Handbook
Seven Levels of Power and Manifestation of the Virgin Mary
Sherrie Dillard
Learn how to invoke the Virgin Mary's presence, communicate with her, receive her grace and miracles and become a miracle worker.
Paperback: 978-1-84694-920-3 ebook: 978-1-84694-921-0

Divine Guidance
The Answers You Need to Make Miracles
Stephanie J. King
Ask any question and the answer will be presented, like a direct line to higher realms… *Divine Guidance* helps you to regain control over your own journey through life.
Paperback: 978-1-78099-794-0 ebook: 978-1-78099-793-3

The End of Death
How Near-Death Experiences Prove the Afterlife
Admir Serrano
A compelling examination of the phenomena of Near-Death
Experiences.
Paperback: 978-1-78279-233-8 ebook: 978-1-78279-232-1

Readers of ebooks can buy or view any of these bestsellers by
clicking on the live link in the title. Most titles are published
in paperback and as an ebook. Paperbacks are available in
traditional bookshops. Both print and ebook formats are available
online.
Find more titles and sign up to our readers' newsletter at
http://www.johnhuntpublishing.com/mind-body-spirit.
Follow us on Facebook at https://www.facebook.com/OBooks
and Twitter at https://twitter.com/obooks.